Natural

Natural

WHOLESOME RECIPES
FOR PURE NOURISHMENT

This edition published by Parragon Books Ltd in 2015
LOVE FOOD is an imprint of Parragon Books Ltd

Parragon Books Ltd
Chartist House
15–17 Trim Street
Bath BA1 1HA, UK
www.parragon.com/lovefood

ISBN 978-1-4723-9243-5
Printed in China

New recipes: Georgina Fuggle
Introduction text: Anne Sheasby
New recipe photography: Mike Cooper
Home economy: Lincoln Jefferson
Cover photography: Haarala Hamilton
Designer: Karli Skelton
Senior Editor: Cheryl Warner
Illustrations: Sarah Dennis, courtesy of New Division agency

NOTES FOR THE READER
This book uses both metric and imperial measurements. Follow the same units of measurement throughout;
do not mix metric and imperial. All spoon measurements are level: teaspoons are assumed to be 5 ml,
and tablespoons are assumed to be 15 ml. Unless otherwise stated, milk is assumed to be full fat, eggs
and individual vegetables are medium, pepper is freshly ground black pepper and salt is table salt. Unless
otherwise stated, all root vegetables should be peeled prior to using.

The times given are an approximate guide only. Preparation times differ according
to the techniques used by different people and the cooking times
may also vary from those given.

Please note that any ingredients stated as being optional, are not included in the nutritional values
provided. The nutritional values given are approximate and provided as a guideline only, they do not
account for individual cooks, scales and portion sizes.

Contents

The Natural Way

Fresh, natural and simple ingredients play an important role in eating well and encourage a clean and health-giving approach to everyday eating. Incorporating more nutrient-dense foods and less processed ones into your everyday diet will also help to boost, balance and benefit your overall health and happiness.

So, forget faddy diets and quick-fix weight-loss plans because here we have the perfect guide to healthy home cooking, the natural way. This inspiring and creative cookbook includes an amazing array of delicious, nutrient-rich recipes to help you feel more energized and revitalized, plus some top tips and savvy solutions for good, simple, natural eating. These recipes include lots of fresh and natural ingredients, as well as a range of superfoods, making them perfect for the healthy home cook who wants to create tasty, nourishing, nutritionally balanced dishes that are ideal for everyday eating. We cater for all tastes and preferences, plus we feature some scrumptious sugar-free, gluten-free and dairy-free options for those needing to avoid certain foods.

A healthy breakfast is important to get you off to a good start as it boosts your energy levels in the morning and improves your ability to concentrate and perform. Therefore, to stimulate your senses first thing, we begin with a super choice of sustaining breakfast recipes including ever-popular porridge and pancakes, plus brilliant blinis, baked eggs, muffins and waffles.

Next, we focus on a tempting assortment of energy-packed lunches that are sure to hit the spot just when your stomach begins to rumble. Appetizing soups, superfood salads, flatbreads, frittatas, wraps, tarts and quiches are all given the spotlight in this chapter.

When energy levels begin to flag during the day, why not turn to our next chapter to discover a savvy selection of super-charged snacks and sides? These are guaranteed to recharge and sustain you until your next meal. Top picks include popcorn, power balls, snacking nuts, roasted chips and wedges, not forgetting fantastic falafels and spiced mash.

Delicious dressings and sauces follow next and these are perfect for adding a beneficial health boost to vibrant salads and wholesome pasta dishes, plus we include some standout dips to enjoy too.

A fabulous feast of versatile vegetable-loaded dishes includes choice cold and hot creations featuring a range of vegetables, beans, rice and pasta, as well as popular grains like farro and seed stars like quinoa.

Power-packed protein dishes include a mouthwatering collection of healthy, balanced recipes from around the world, boasting nutrient-rich salads and stir-fries, hearty roasts and grills, plus some feel-good couscous creations.

A scrumptious selection of healthy desserts and bakes promises plenty of appealing recipes to satisfy those sweet cravings. Temptations range from family favourites like crumbles, brownies and cupcakes, to chilled or frozen sensations such as cheesecakes, mousses and sundaes.

Finally, to finish things off on a healthy high note, we showcase some nourishing nectars that are ideal for refreshing and revitalizing. We include invigorating juices, tonics, coolers, whips and milkshakes, as well as some restorative teas and infusions.

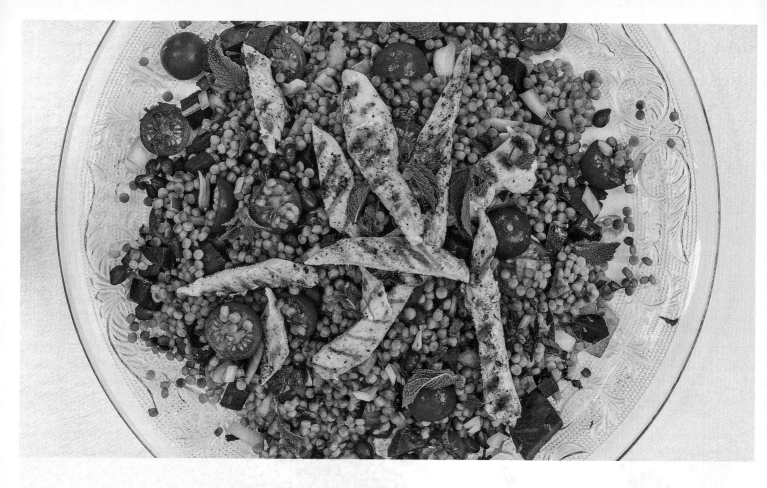

Nourish and Cleanse

Explore the diverse selection of simple, natural, healthy foods that are readily available, and aim to include a good variety of these foods in your everyday eating plan. Include lean meats, white fish, oily fish, a variety of beans and pulses, plenty of fruit and vegetables (at least five different portions every day), some whole dairy foods as well as soya or other dairy-free alternatives, whole grains, rice and pasta, eggs, nuts and seeds. Herbs and spices add an arsenal of clean, natural flavours to many dishes too.

Aim to eat an assortment of different coloured fruits and vegetables, including a number of those high in antioxidants such as beetroot, berries (for example blackberries, blueberries and raspberries), broccoli, cherries, kale, red grapes, red peppers, spinach, tomatoes, and so on.

Healthier choices of grains include fibre-rich brown rice, wholewheat pasta, whole grain flours and wholemeal bread. Or occasionally opt for things like barley, buckwheat, quinoa and farro to add interest and variety to your meals.

Nuts are packed with protein, plus they provide a variety of valuable vitamins and minerals, and although nuts are typically high in fat, the fats tend to be the more healthy unsaturated types. Seeds, such as pumpkin, sunflower, sesame, chia and linseeds, add a nourishing nutrient boost to dishes too. For the sweet stuff, choose unrefined brown sugars instead of refined white ones, if you can.

If you are a meat or fish eater, then choose leaner cuts of meat and poultry and include both white fish and oily fish in your diet (oily fish are an excellent source of omega-3 fatty acids).

For vegetarians, beans and pulses provide an important source of protein, as well as fibre and vital vitamins and minerals, and a good range of dried, canned, fresh and frozen ones are readily available. Or, if you want to eat less meat and fancy meat-light or meat-free days, then beans and pulses are great for bulking out dishes such as casseroles, soups and salads.

For health-conscious eaters, cooking from scratch really lends itself to natural home cooking as it enables you to select the ingredients you want to use. Be label-aware though and become a savvy shopper, because even with home-made food, some ingredients may be processed. Certain processed foods can be eaten as part of a healthy, natural diet (for example, canned vegetables and beans without added sugar and salt), but many processed foods contain added sugar, salt and fat (especially saturated fat) in varying amounts. So before you set off shopping and make your choices, check out the general guidelines readily available and get accustomed to checking the labels before you buy.

This appealing collection of flavourful, wholesome recipes will inspire and spur you on to embrace a healthy, natural and balanced approach to eating for improved overall vitality and well-being. We include lots of delicious and satisfying recipes for all tastes that will effortlessly slot into a nourishing everyday diet, so you can easily enjoy cooking and eating delicious feel-good food packed full of fresh flavour and appeal.

Naturally Good Ingredients

Many of us are familiar with foods that are considered to have superfood status like avocados, spinach, blueberries, and so on, but there are other ingredients that also pack a powerful nutritional punch and provide wide-ranging nutrients and health benefits. These A-list ingredients are the perfect choice for creating delicious dishes using naturally good foods, and they are becoming increasingly readily available in supermarkets, as well as in health food shops, delis and online. We include the scoop on some of these on-trend powerhouse foods...

Almond milk - Made by toasting or roasting whole almonds, then grinding them and blending with water. A dairy-free alternative to traditional dairy milk; naturally low in fat, lactose-free, gluten-free and cholesterol-free.

Beetroot - Deep red beetroot are the most common, but pink, golden and stripy beetroot are also available. Low in fat and packed full of vitamins, minerals and antioxidants; good source of fibre.

Buckwheat - Comprising grain-like triangular seeds (that are no relation to cereal wheat) with a nutty flavour; can be used toasted or plain, as whole seeds or ground into flour. Good source of protein and fibre; naturally gluten-free and wheat-free.

Chia seeds - Tiny, oval, mottled brown/grey seeds. Natural, rich, gluten-free source of omega-3 fatty acids; good source of vitamins, minerals, protein and fibre.

Coconut oil - Very high in saturated fats, but the type of saturated fatty acids it contains (which differ from those typically found in animal products) are considered to be 'good' saturated fats. However, use in moderation.

Coconut water - Clear liquid extracted from the inside of young green coconuts. A good source of important vitamins and minerals, including potassium; low in calories and fat (and cholesterol-free).

Goji berries - Small, shrivelled, dried vibrant red berries; contain a variety of valuable vitamins and minerals, including antioxidants.

Kale - Member of cabbage family. Hardy, deep green, leafy winter vegetable with strong flavour; available as smooth-leaved kale or crinkly-leaved curly kale. Excellent source of various vitamins and minerals, including vitamin C.

Linseeds - Small, pale brown or golden seeds; also known as flaxseeds. Naturally gluten-free; rich source of omega-3 essential fatty acids and good source of fibre.

Medjool dates - Large, fleshy dates imported from Middle East and North Africa; available all year round. Low in fat and sodium; good source of fibre. Very high natural sugar content.

Pomegranate - Inside the hard, red-blushed skin are numerous edible seeds, each one surrounded by a sac of sweet, juicy, vibrant pink flesh (packed in bitter white pith). Low in fat; good source of fibre, antioxidant vitamins and minerals.

Quinoa - Ancient grain-like seed from South America. Tiny, round, bead-shaped seeds, available in three main types (red, creamy white/pale golden and black); swell up as they cook and have a mild, nutty taste. Complete protein food (contains all essential amino acids). Good gluten-free source of protein, fibre and minerals.

Spirulina - Blue-green natural freshwater algae, rich in protein (complete protein food – contains all essential amino acids) and other nutrients, including various vitamins and minerals. Available as a nutrient-dense powder (or tablets).

Wheatgrass - Available fresh or as a juice or powder. Fresh wheatgrass is grown from sprouted wheatgrass seeds or wheat berries; vibrant green in colour, with a strong, sweet, grass-like flavour. Natural, rich source of vitamins and minerals, including antioxidants.

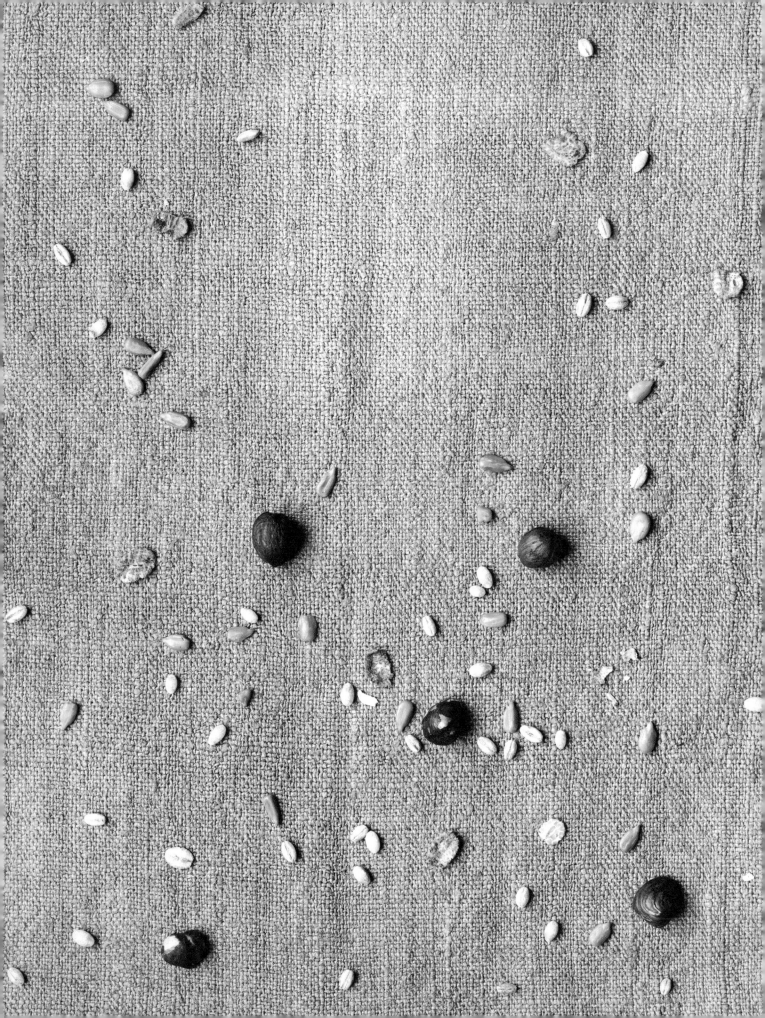

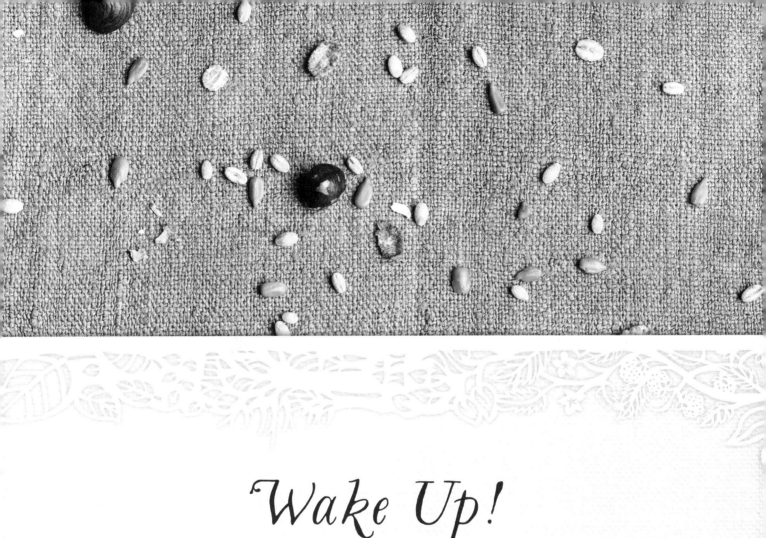

Wake Up!

Barley Porridge with Grilled Fruits

This maca-enriched creamy barley porridge is made with almond milk and topped with cinnamon-caramelized grilled fresh peaches and papaya. It is then drizzled with honey to create this tasty, dairy-free breakfast.

Serves 4

Prep: 15 minutes
Cook: 10–15 minutes

85 g/3 oz barley flakes
85 g/3 oz porridge oats
350 ml/12 fl oz cold water
750 ml/1¼ pints unsweetened almond milk
4 tsp maca
2 peaches, halved, stoned and sliced
1 papaya, halved, deseeded, peeled and sliced
4 tsp runny honey
½ tsp ground cinnamon
2 tsp runny honey, to serve

1. Put the barley flakes, porridge oats, water and almond milk in a saucepan. Bring to the boil over a medium–high heat, then reduce the heat to medium and simmer for 5–10 minutes, stirring often, until soft and thickened. Stir in the maca.

2. Meanwhile, preheat the grill to medium–high. Line the grill rack with foil, then lay the peaches and papaya on top, drizzle with the honey and sprinkle with the cinnamon. Grill for 3–4 minutes, or until hot and just beginning to caramelize.

3. Spoon the porridge into bowls, top with the hot peaches and papaya and drizzle with the honey.

PER SERVING: 280 Kcals / 4.3g fat / 0.5g sat fat / 53.6g carbs / 20.8g sugar / 9.4g fibre / 7.8g protein / 0.2g salt

Greek-style Yogurt with Orange Zest & Toasted Seeds

<u>Serves 2</u>
Prep: 10 minutes, plus cooling
Cook: 2–3 minutes

2 tsp linseeds
2 tsp pumpkin seeds
2 tsp chia seeds
200 g/7 oz Greek-style natural yogurt
grated zest of 1 small
   orange, plus 1 tsp juice

Nutritious assorted seeds add extra crunch, flavour and colour to these quick and easy low-sugar yogurt pots.

1. Place a small frying pan over a medium heat. When it is hot, tip in the seeds. Toast, stirring constantly with a wooden spoon, until they start to turn brown and release a nutty aroma. Tip them on to a plate and leave to cool.

2. Spoon the yogurt into two glass pots or serving bowls, then scatter the seeds on top, followed by the orange zest. Sprinkle over the orange juice and serve immediately.

PER SERVING: *152 Kcals / 8.9g fat / 4g sat fat / 7.7g carbs / 4.1g sugar / 2.7g fibre / 11.1g protein / 0.1g salt*

Healthy French Toast with Bananas & Toasted Pecans

Serves 4

Prep: 20 minutes
Cook: 12–17 minutes

60 g/2¼ oz pecan nuts,
    roughly chopped
2 eggs
4 ripe bananas, chopped
½ tsp vanilla extract
½ tsp ground cinnamon
4 slices thick wholemeal bread
1 tbsp olive oil
½ tsp ground cinnamon, to sprinkle

There's no better way to start the day than with this very tempting, sustaining banana-and-nut-topped French toast.

1. Place the pecans into a small, dry frying pan and toast over a medium heat for 3–4 minutes, tossing regularly until just toasted. Set aside.

2. Place the eggs, 2 bananas, vanilla extract and cinnamon into a blender and whizz for 1–2 minutes, or until the consistency is smooth and thick.

3. Pour the mixture into a medium, shallow dish. Place two slices of bread into the mixture and, working quickly, gently press the bread into the liquid, allowing it to soak up the mixture. Turn the slices over and repeat.

4. Meanwhile, heat half of the olive oil in a large, non-stick frying pan over a medium–high heat. Using a spatula, remove the soaked bread from the banana mixture and place in the frying pan. Cook for 2–3 minutes on each side before removing from the pan. Repeat the process for the remaining slices, adding the remaining olive oil if needed.

5. Serve the banana bread immediately, with a sprinkling of cinnamon and the toasted pecans and two chopped bananas on top.

PER SERVING: *405 Kcals / 19.4g fat / 2.7g sat fat / 53.4g carbs / 17g sugar / 7.6g fibre / 9.7g protein / 0.5g salt*

Super Seedy Granola

For a satisfying start to the day, try this great-tasting granola, heaped with healthy cinnamon-toasted wholegrain oats and seeds and combined with fibre-rich dried fruits. Make ahead as it keeps for a few days too.

Serves 6

Prep: 20 minutes, plus cooling and storing
Cook: 30–35 minutes

150 g/5½ oz porridge oats
40 g/1½ oz pumpkin seeds
40 g/1½ oz sunflower seeds
40 g/1½ oz sesame seeds
1 tsp ground cinnamon
2 tbsp light muscovado sugar
2 tbsp olive oil
2 tbsp runny honey
juice of 1 small orange
40 g/1½ oz dried apple slices, diced
40 g/1½ oz dried blueberries
40 g/1½ oz dried cranberries

1. Preheat the oven to 160°C/325°F/Gas Mark 3. Add the oats, pumpkin seeds, sunflower seeds and sesame seeds to an 18 x 28-cm/7 x 11-inch roasting tin. Sprinkle with the cinnamon and sugar, and stir together.

2. Drizzle the oil, honey and orange juice over the top and mix together. Bake in the preheated oven for 30–35 minutes, stirring after 15 minutes, moving the mix in the corners to the centre as the edges brown more quickly. Try to keep the granola in clumps. Return to the oven and stir every 5–10 minutes, until the granola is an even, golden brown.

3. Scatter the dried apple, blueberries and cranberries over the top and leave the granola to cool and harden. Serve or spoon into a plastic container or preserving jar and store in the refrigerator for up to 4 days.

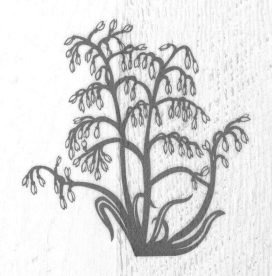

PER SERVING: *357 Kcals / 16.3g fat / 2.3g sat fat / 48.4g carbs / 23.3g sugar / 6.2g fibre / 8.2g protein / trace salt*

Spinach & Nutmeg Baked Eggs

Serves 4
Prep: 20 minutes, plus cooling
Cook: 20–30 minutes

1 tbsp olive oil, for brushing
1 tbsp olive oil, for frying
4 shallots, finely chopped
3 garlic cloves, sliced
100 g/3½ oz baby spinach
8 eggs
½ tsp ground nutmeg
salt and pepper, optional

Nutrient-rich fresh spinach adds delicious flavour and colour to this popular egg dish, lightly seasoned with ground nutmeg. Serve with standard or gluten-free bread for a wholesome breakfast or brunch.

1. Preheat the oven to 180°C/350°F/Gas Mark 4. Lightly brush the insides of four 200 ml/7 fl oz ramekins with olive oil.

2. Heat the olive oil in a frying pan. Once hot, add the shallots and garlic and fry over a medium heat for 3–4 minutes, or until soft. Add the baby spinach and stir for 2–3 minutes, or until just wilted. Season with salt and pepper, if using.

3. Spoon the spinach mixture into the bottom of the prepared ramekins and crack two eggs into each. Sprinkle over the nutmeg and place the ramekins in a roasting tin. Fill the roasting tin with boiling water until the water reaches halfway up the ramekins – this creates a steamy environment for the eggs so there is no chance of them drying out.

4. Carefully transfer the roasting tin to the preheated oven for 15–20 minutes. Leave the ramekins to cool slightly then serve immediately.

PER SERVING: *235 Kcals / 16.5g fat / 4.2g sat fat / 7.5g carbs / 1.6g sugar / 1.1g fibre / 14.2g protein / 0.4g salt*

Cinnamon Pancakes with Tropical Fruit Salad

Using soya milk for these tasty wholemeal pancakes, and serving them with soya yogurt, ensures they are delicious and dairy-free. Naturally sweet ripe pineapple and mango means no sugar is needed for the fruit salad.

Serves 4
Prep: 30 minutes
Cook: 30 minutes

100 g/3½ oz wholemeal plain flour
½ tsp ground cinnamon
2 eggs, beaten
225 ml/8 fl oz unsweetened soya milk
3 tbsp water
3 tbsp sunflower oil

Fruit salad
1 ruby grapefruit
250 g/9 oz pineapple flesh, cut into cubes
150 g/5½ oz mango flesh, cut into cubes
finely grated zest of ½ lime

To serve
300 g/10½ oz natural soya yogurt
2 tbsp date syrup
40 g/1½ oz Brazil nuts, roughly chopped, optional

1. For the fruit salad, cut the peel and pith away from the grapefruit with a small serrated knife. Hold it above a bowl and cut between the membranes to release the segments into the bowl. Squeeze the juice from the membranes into the bowl. Add the pineapple, mango and lime zest and mix well.

2. For the pancakes, put the flour and cinnamon in another bowl. Add the eggs, then gradually whisk in the soya milk until smooth. Whisk in the water and 1 tablespoon of oil.

PER SERVING: *369 Kcals / 16.2g fat / 2.4g sat fat / 45.9g carbs / 22.3g sugar / 6.4g fibre / 12.5g protein / 0.3g salt*

3. Heat a little oil in an 18-cm/7-inch frying pan over a medium heat, then pour out the excess oil. Pour in one-eighth of the batter, tilting the pan to swirl the batter into an even layer. Cook for 2 minutes, or until the underside is golden.

4. Loosen the pancake, then flip it over with a palette knife and cook the second side for 1 minute, or until golden. Slide the pancake out of the pan and keep hot on a plate while you make seven more thin pancakes in the same way.

5. Arrange two folded pancakes on each of four plates and top with the fruit salad. Serve with the soya yogurt and drizzle with the date syrup. Top with the Brazil nuts, if using.

Breakfast Carrot Cake Biscuits

Makes 12

Prep: 25–30 minutes
Cook: 16–19 minutes

100 g/3½ oz linseeds
85 g/3 oz wholemeal plain flour
70 g/2½ oz porridge oats
1 tsp baking powder
1 tsp ground ginger
2 tsp ground cinnamon
85 g/3 oz dried apricots,
    finely chopped
1 dessert apple, cored
    and coarsely grated
1 carrot, finely grated
40 g/1½ oz pecan nuts,
    roughly chopped
3 tbsp coconut oil
125 ml/4 fl oz maple syrup
grated zest of ½ orange,
    plus 3 tbsp juice
4 tbsp dried coconut shavings

Full of nutrient-loaded seeds, oats, nuts, carrots and fruit, these lightly spiced zesty biscuits pack a fantastic flavour punch, as well as being great for energy. They are perfect for breakfast on the run as they can be made ahead too.

1. Preheat the oven to 180°C/350°F/ Gas Mark 4 and line two baking sheets with baking paper.

2. Put the linseeds in a blender and process to a fine powder, then tip into a mixing bowl. Add the flour, oats and baking powder, then the ginger and cinnamon, and stir well. Add the dried apricots, apple, carrot and pecan nuts and stir again.

3. Warm the coconut oil in a small saucepan (or in the microwave for 30 seconds) until just liquid. Remove from the heat, then stir in the maple syrup and orange zest and juice. Pour this into the carrot mixture and stir until you have a soft dough.

4. Spoon 12 mounds of the mixture onto the prepared baking sheets, then flatten them into thick 7.5-cm/3-inch diameter rounds. Sprinkle with the coconut shavings, then bake in the preheated oven for 15–18 minutes, or until browned.

5. Serve warm or leave to cool, then pack into a plastic container and store in the fridge for up to 3 days.

PER BISCUIT: 212 Kcals / 11.2g fat / 4.7g sat fat / 27g carbs / 12.4g sugar / 5.5g fibre / 4.1g protein / 0.1g salt

Three Herb & Ricotta Omelette

Vibrant green mixed garden herbs add lots of lovely natural flavour and colour to this appetizing omelette. Served with fresh bread to accompany, it's just the ticket for a satisfying breakfast for two.

Serves 2
Prep: 15 minutes
Cook: 8 minutes

4 large eggs
2 tbsp finely snipped fresh chives
2 tbsp finely chopped fresh basil
2 tbsp finely chopped fresh parsley
100 g/3½ oz ricotta cheese, crumbled
2 tbsp olive oil
salt and pepper, optional

1. Crack the eggs into a small mixing bowl and lightly beat with a fork. Stir the herbs and ricotta into the bowl and season with salt and pepper, if using.

2. Heat the olive oil in a non-stick frying pan over a high heat until hot. Pour in the egg mixture and, using a spatula, draw the outside edges (which will cook more quickly) towards the gooey centre. Allow any liquid mixture to move into the gaps. Continue with this action for about 4–5 minutes. The omelette will continue to cook once the pan is removed from the heat.

3. Cut the omelette in half and divide between two plates. Serve immediately.

PER SERVING: 390 Kcals / 32g fat / 10g sat fat / 2.8g carbs / 0.7g sugar / 0.2g fibre / 21.7g protein / 0.6g salt

Home-made Cacao & Hazelnut Butter

Makes 225 g / 8 oz
Prep: 15 minutes, plus standing
Cook: 3–4 minutes

115 g/4 oz unblanched hazelnuts
25 g/1 oz raw cacao powder
70 g/2½ oz light muscovado sugar
125 ml/4 fl oz light olive oil
½ tsp vanilla extract
pinch of sea salt
wholegrain toast or pancakes,
  to serve, optional

Spread on hot wholegrain toast, this healthy hazelnut butter is delicious for breakfast, plus it keeps well for several days.

1. Add the hazelnuts to a dry frying pan and cook over a medium heat for 3–4 minutes, constantly shaking the pan, until the nuts are an even golden brown in colour.

2. Wrap the nuts in a clean tea towel and rub to remove the skins.

3. Put the nuts into a blender and blend until finely ground. Add the cacao powder, sugar, oil, vanilla extract and salt, and blend again to make a smooth paste.

4. Spoon into a small preserving jar and clip the lid in place. Leave to stand at room temperature for 4 hours, until the sugar has dissolved completely. Stir again, then store in the refrigerator for up to 5 days. Serve on wholegrain toast or hot pancakes, if desired.

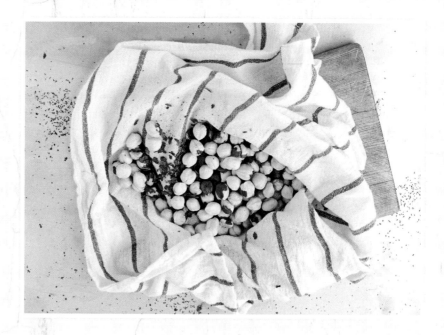

PER 225 G/8 OZ: *2206 Kcals / 197.7g fat / 24.2g sat fat / 104.3g carbs / 73.2g sugar / 18.3g fibre / 22.7g protein / 1.5g salt*

Cardamom Waffles with Blackberries & Figs

Aromatic cardamom adds a wonderful depth of flavour to these fabulous fruit-topped waffles, so dig out your waffle maker and cook up this satisfying weekend family breakfast when late-summer blackberries are at their best.

Serves 6
Prep: 25 minutes, plus resting
Cook: 10–17 minutes

5 large eggs, separated
pinch of salt
1 tsp ground cardamom
50 g/1¾ oz unsalted butter, melted and cooled
250 ml/9 fl oz semi-skimmed milk
225 g/8 oz wholemeal plain flour
1 tbsp olive oil, for brushing
150 g/5½ oz Greek-style natural yogurt
6 ripe figs, quartered
200 g/7 oz blackberries
6 tbsp agave syrup, to serve

1. Place the egg yolks, salt and cardamom into a bowl and beat well with a wooden spoon. Stir in the melted butter. Slowly beat in the milk until fully incorporated. Gradually add the flour until you have a thick batter.

2. In a separate bowl, whisk the egg whites until they form stiff peaks and gently fold them into the batter. Leave the batter to rest for at least an hour, but preferably overnight.

3. Heat the waffle maker according to the manufacturers' instructions. Brush with a little oil and spoon the batter onto the waffle iron. Cook for 4–5 minutes, or until golden. Keep each waffle warm, under foil, in a low oven until you are ready to serve.

4. Serve each waffle immediately, topped with yogurt, fig quarters, blackberries and agave syrup.

PER SERVING: *422 Kcals / 17.3g fat / 7.8g sat fat / 53.9g carbs / 23.7g sugar / 7.3g fibre / 16.1g protein / 0.5g salt*

Pumpkin & Pepita Muffins

Makes 12
Prep: 25–30 minutes, plus cooling
Cook: 30 minutes

1 tbsp light olive oil, for greasing
250 g/9 oz peeled,
    deseeded pumpkin, finely diced
4-cm/1½-inch piece fresh ginger,
    coarsely grated
3 eggs
4 tbsp maple syrup
225 ml/8 fl oz low-fat
    natural yogurt
150 g/5½ oz wholemeal plain flour
100 g/3½ oz fine cornmeal
3 tsp baking powder
1 tsp ground mixed spice
3 tbsp pepita (pumpkin) seeds

Dark olive-green pepita (pumpkin) seeds add crunch and a mild nutty flavour to these moreish muffins. They are ideal for an energy-boosting breakfast or brunch and are great as a mid-morning snack.

1. Preheat the oven to 190°C/375°F/Gas Mark 5. Grease a 12-hole muffin tin with the oil.

2. Place the pumpkin in the top of a steamer set over a saucepan of gently simmering water. Cover and cook for 15 minutes, or until just soft. Mash the pumpkin and mix with the grated ginger.

3. Place the eggs, maple syrup and yogurt in a medium-sized bowl and whisk together.

4. Put the flour, cornmeal, baking powder and mixed spice into a large bowl and stir together. Add the mashed pumpkin and egg mixture and briefly whisk together until just combined.

5. Spoon the mixture evenly into the holes of the prepared tin. Sprinkle the tops of the muffins with the seeds, then bake in the preheated oven for 15 minutes, or until well risen and golden brown. Leave to cool in the tin for 5 minutes, then loosen the edges with a knife. Turn out onto a wire rack and leave to cool completely.

PER MUFFIN: *150 Kcals / 4.2g fat / 1g sat fat / 23.7g carbs / 5.9g sugar / 1.9g fibre / 5.7g protein / 0.4g salt*

Red Beetroot Hash

Serves 4

Prep: 25–30 minutes

Cook: 45 minutes

350 g/12 oz Jerusalem artichokes,
   unpeeled and scrubbed

450 g/1 lb raw beetroot, cut into cubes

750 g/1 lb 10 oz sweet
   potatoes, cut into cubes

2 tbsp olive oil

1 red onion, roughly chopped

2 tsp mild paprika

½ tsp mustard powder

3 tsp fresh thyme leaves

4 eggs

salt and pepper, optional

1 tsp fresh thyme leaves, to garnish

Heaped with health-giving nutrients, fresh beetroot adds wonderful colour and flavour to this wholesome root vegetable hash, topped with protein-rich eggs. An ideal meat-free weekend breakfast or brunch for the whole family.

1. Halve any of the larger artichokes. Half-fill the base of a steamer with water, bring to the boil, then add the artichokes to the water. Put the beetroot in one half of the steamer top, cover with a lid and steam for 10 minutes.

2. Put the sweet potatoes in the other half of the top, so the colour of the beetroot won't bleed into the sweet potatoes. Cover with a lid again and steam for 10 minutes more, or until all the vegetables are just tender. Drain the artichokes, peel them and cut them into cubes.

3. Heat 1 tablespoon of oil in a large frying pan over a medium heat. Add the red onion and fry for 3–4 minutes, or until beginning to soften. Add the artichokes, beetroot and sweet potatoes and fry for 10 minutes, or until browned.

4. Stir in the paprika, mustard powder and thyme and season with salt and pepper, if using. Make four spaces in the frying pan, drizzle in the remaining oil, then crack an egg into each hole. Sprinkle the eggs with salt and pepper, if using, then cover and cook for 4–5 minutes, or until the eggs are cooked to your liking. Spoon onto plates and serve immediately, garnished with the thyme.

PER SERVING: *426 Kcals / 12.1g fat / 2.6g sat fat / 68.5g carbs / 25.7g sugar / 11.3g fibre / 13.4g protein / 0.6g salt*

Mushrooms on Rye Toast

Simple to make and very tasty, these mixed fresh mushrooms are pan-fried with garlic, then served on top of toasted rye bread, which creates a quick and easy breakfast to get you off to a good start in the morning.

Serves 4
Prep: 15 minutes
Cook: 10 minutes

3 tbsp olive oil
2 large garlic cloves, crushed
225 g/8 oz chestnut mushrooms, sliced
225 g/8 oz wild mushrooms, sliced
2 tsp lemon juice
2 tbsp finely chopped fresh flat-leaf parsley
4 slices of rye bread
sea salt and pepper, optional

1. Heat the oil in a large frying pan over a medium–low heat. Add the garlic and cook for a few seconds.

2. Increase the heat to high. Add the chestnut mushrooms to the pan and cook, stirring continuously, for 3 minutes. Add the wild mushrooms and cook for a further 2 minutes.

3. Stir in the lemon juice and parsley, and season with salt and pepper, if using.

4. Lightly toast the rye bread then transfer to a serving plate. Spoon the mushroom mixture over the toast and serve immediately.

PER SERVING: 206 Kcals / 11.6g fat / 1.6g sat fat / 21.8g carbs / 2.6g sugar / 3.9g fibre / 6.1g protein / 0.9g salt

Buckwheat Blinis with Pears & Blueberries

Serves 4
Prep: 30 minutes, plus rising
Cook: 20–27 minutes

175 g/6 oz buckwheat flour
½ tsp sea salt
2 tsp dark muscovado sugar
1 tsp easy-blend dried yeast
125 ml/4 fl oz milk
125 ml/4 fl oz water
1 tbsp virgin olive oil

Topping

25 g/1 oz unsalted butter
2 pears, cored and thickly sliced
150 g/5½ oz blueberries
2 tbsp runny honey
juice of ½ lemon
200 g/7 oz Greek-style natural yogurt
pinch of ground cinnamon
25 g/1 oz toasted unblanched
  hazelnuts, roughly chopped

Superfood blueberries are a rich source of antioxidants and, when cooked lightly with pears, they provide a tasty topping for these naturally gluten-free buckwheat blinis. Greek-style yogurt and toasted hazelnuts complete this healthy breakfast perfectly.

1. To make the blinis, put the flour, salt, sugar and yeast in a large bowl and mix together well. Place the milk and water in a small saucepan and gently heat until just warm. Gradually whisk the milk mixture into the flour until you have a smooth, thick batter.

2. Cover the bowl with a large plate and leave it in a warm place to rise for 40–60 minutes, or until bubbles appear on the surface and the batter is almost doubled in size.

3. Heat half of the oil in a large griddle pan over a medium heat. Remove the pan from the heat briefly and wipe away excess oil using kitchen paper. Return the pan to the heat and drop dessertspoons of the batter into it, leaving a little space between them. Cook for 2–3 minutes, or until the undersides are golden and the tops are beginning to bubble.

4. Turn the blinis over with a spatula and cook for 1–2 minutes more. Transfer them to a baking sheet and keep warm in the oven while you make the rest. Continue wiping the pan with oiled kitchen paper between cooking batches.

5. To make the topping, melt the butter in a frying pan over a medium heat. Add the fruit and cook for 2–3 minutes, or until hot. Drizzle over the honey and lemon juice and cook for 1 minute, or until the blueberry juices begin to run.

6. Arrange three blinis on each of four plates, top with spoonfuls of the yogurt, the hot fruit, a little ground cinnamon and the hazelnuts. Serve immediately.

PER SERVING: 435 Kcals / 17g fat / 6.4g sat fat / 64.1g carbs / 27.1g sugar / 8.5g fibre / 13g protein / 0.8g salt

Poached Eggs & Kale with Wholemeal Sourdough

Serves 4
Prep: 20 minutes
Cook: 15–17 minutes

4 eggs

100 g/3½ oz kale, chopped

4 large slices wholemeal
    sourdough bread

2 garlic cloves, chopped into halves

2 tbsp olive oil

1 tsp dried red chilli flakes

salt and pepper, optional

Kale adds valuable nutrients and vivid green colour to these protein-packed poached eggs served on sensational sourdough toast.

1. Begin by poaching the eggs. Bring a shallow saucepan of water to a gentle simmer. Crack an egg into a small bowl or ramekin, then slide the egg into the water, lowering the bowl as close to the water as possible. Using a large spoon, gently fold any stray strands of white around the yolk. Repeat with the other eggs.

2. Cook for 2–3 minutes, or until set to your liking, then remove with a slotted spoon. Place the eggs in a small bowl of warm water so they can sit until needed.

3. Bring a saucepan of water to the boil and add the kale. Simmer for 3–4 minutes, or until the kale is just cooked but still retains a little crunch. Drain, season with salt and pepper, if using, and set aside.

4. Meanwhile, toast the sourdough bread. Place the toast on four plates, then rub each slice with the raw garlic and drizzle with the olive oil. Top the toast with the blanched kale and a poached egg. Finally sprinkle over chilli flakes. Serve immediately.

PER SERVING: *324 Kcals / 15.1g fat / 3g sat fat / 36.3g carbs / 2.6g sugar / 4.4g fibre / 12.6g protein / 1g salt*

Banana, Goji & Hazelnut Bread

Bananas are a storehouse of beneficial nutrients, so when you want to feel energized first thing, try this healthy, high-fibre breakfast loaf packed with bananas and dotted with nutritious goji berries and hazelnuts throughout.

Serves 10

Prep: 25 minutes, plus cooling
Cook: 50–60 minutes

10 g/¼ oz butter, for greasing
85 g/3 oz butter, softened
115 g/4 oz light muscovado sugar
2 eggs
3 bananas (500 g/1 lb 2 oz with the skins on),
    peeled and mashed
115 g/4 oz wholemeal plain flour
115 g/4 oz plain flour
2 tsp baking powder
55 g/2 oz unblanched hazelnuts, roughly chopped
40 g/1½ oz goji berries
40 g/1½ oz dried banana chips

1. Preheat the oven to 180°C/350°F/Gas Mark 4. Grease a 900-g/2-lb loaf tin and line the base and two long sides with a piece of baking paper.

2. Cream the butter and sugar together in a large bowl. Beat in the eggs, one at a time, then the bananas.

3. Put the flours and baking powder in a bowl and mix well. Add to the banana mixture and beat until smooth. Add the hazelnuts and goji berries and stir well.

4. Spoon the mixture into the prepared tin, smooth the top flat then sprinkle with the banana chips. Bake for 50–60 minutes, or until the loaf is well risen, has cracked slightly and a skewer comes out cleanly when inserted into the centre.

5. Leave to cool for 5 minutes, then loosen the edges with a round-bladed knife and turn out onto a wire rack. Leave to cool completely, then peel away the paper. Store in an airtight tin for up to 3 days.

PER SERVING: 300 Kcals / 12.8g fat / 5.6g sat fat / 43.4g carbs / 19.3g sugar / 3.7g fibre / 5.9g protein / 0.4g salt

Walnut & Seed Bread

Makes 2 large loaves

Prep: 30–35 minutes,
 plus rising and cooling
Cook: 25–30 minutes

450 g/1 lb wholemeal plain flour
450 g/1 lb granary plain flour
115 g/4 oz strong white flour
2 tbsp sesame seeds
2 tbsp sunflower seeds
2 tbsp poppy seeds
115 g/4 oz walnuts, chopped
2 tsp salt
15 g/½ oz easy-blend dried yeast
2 tbsp walnut oil
700 ml/1¼ pints lukewarm water
2 tbsp strong white flour,
 for dusting
1 tbsp melted butter, for greasing

Wholesome walnuts and scrumptious seeds add top flavour and crunch to this tempting wholegrain loaf. It's good served thickly sliced and spread with a little honey or soft cheese for a filling, healthy breakfast.

1. Put the flours, seeds, walnuts, salt and yeast into a bowl and mix together. Make a well in the centre, add the oil and water and stir well to form a soft dough. Turn out the dough onto a lightly floured surface and knead well for 5–7 minutes, or until smooth and elastic.

2. Return the dough to the bowl, cover with a damp tea towel and leave in a warm place for 1–1½ hours to rise, or until doubled in size. Turn out onto a lightly floured surface and knead again for 1 minute.

3. Brush two 900-g/2-lb loaf tins well with melted butter. Divide the dough in two. Shape one piece the length of the tin and three times the width. Fold the dough in three lengthways and place in one of the tins with the join underneath. Repeat with the other piece of dough.

4. Cover and leave to rise again in a warm place for about 30 minutes, or until well risen above the tins. Meanwhile, preheat the oven to 230°C/450°F/Gas Mark 8.

5. Bake the loaves in the centre of the preheated oven for 25–30 minutes. If the loaves are getting too brown, reduce the temperature to 220°C/425°F/Gas Mark 7. Transfer to wire racks to cool.

PER LOAF: 3053 Kcals / 83.8g fat / 12.4g sat fat / 480g carbs / 12g sugar / 52g fibre / 114g protein / 6.1g salt

Energy-fuelling Lunches

Smashed Avocado & Quinoa Wrap

Brimming with nourishing, natural goodness, fresh avocado and spinach combine with colourful, crunchy raw red cabbage to create these really appealing quinoa-topped wraps. Great for sharing as everyone can assemble their own.

Serves 4

Prep: 20 minutes, plus cooling
Cook: 15–18 minutes

175 g/6 oz quinoa
400 ml/14 fl oz vegetable stock
1 large, ripe avocado, peeled and stoned
½ tsp smoked paprika
2 garlic cloves, crushed
grated zest and juice of 1 lemon
4 wholemeal tortillas
50 g/1¾ oz baby spinach
150 g/5½ oz red cabbage, finely sliced
salt and pepper, optional

1. Place the quinoa and vegetable stock in a small saucepan and simmer, covered, for 15–18 minutes, or until the stock has been fully absorbed. Set aside to cool.

2. Meanwhile gently mash the avocado flesh with the smoked paprika, crushed garlic, lemon zest and just enough lemon juice to make a thick consistency.

3. Spread the mashed avocado down the centre of each wrap and then top with the warm quinoa, spinach and red cabbage. Season with salt and pepper, if using. Tuck in the ends and tightly fold or roll into a wrap and serve immediately.

PER SERVING: *385 Kcals / 13.2g fat / 2.8g sat fat / 56.8g carbs / 3.6g sugar / 10.4g fibre / 11.8g protein / 1.4g salt*

Super Green Salad

Serves 4
Prep: 20–25 minutes
Cook: 10–14 minutes

2 tbsp pumpkin seeds
2 tbsp sunflower seeds
2 tbsp sesame seeds
4 tsp soy sauce
250 g/9 oz broccoli, cut into florets
85 g/3 oz baby spinach
55 g/2 oz kale, thinly shredded
15 g/½ oz fresh coriander,
  roughly chopped
2 avocados, sliced
juice of 2 limes

Dressing
3 tbsp flaxseed oil
2 tsp runny honey
pepper, optional

This vibrant green superfood salad is sure to hit the spot when you are looking for a healthy but substantial meal at lunchtime. Serve the salad simply on its own or with some wholemeal bread or wholegrain crackers.

1. Place a frying pan over a high heat. Add the pumpkin, sunflower and sesame seeds, cover and dry-fry for 3–4 minutes, or until lightly toasted and beginning to pop, shaking the pan from time to time. Remove from the heat and stir in the soy sauce.

2. Half-fill the base of a steamer with water, bring to the boil, then put the broccoli in the steamer top. Cover with a lid and steam for 3–5 minutes, or until tender. Transfer to a salad bowl and add the spinach, kale and coriander.

3. Put the avocados and half of the lime juice in a small bowl and toss well, then tip them into the salad bowl.

4. To make the dressing, put the remaining lime juice, the oil, honey and pepper, if using, in a small jug and whisk together. Sprinkle the toasted seeds over the salad and serve immediately, with the dressing alongside for pouring.

PER SERVING: *343 Kcals / 28.6g fat / 3.5g sat fat / 20.4g carbs / 5.2g sugar / 8.8g fibre / 8g protein / 0.9g salt*

Wholemeal Spinach, Pea & Feta Tart

Serves 6
Prep: 35 minutes,
  plus chilling and cooling
Cook: 1–1¼ hours

15 g/½ oz unsalted butter
3 spring onions, thinly sliced
200 g/7 oz baby spinach
100 g/3½ oz podded peas
3 eggs
250 ml/9 fl oz milk
100 g/3½ oz feta cheese,
  finely crumbled
115 g/4 oz cherry tomatoes
salt and pepper, optional

Pastry
115 g/4 oz unsalted
  butter, cut into cubes
225 g/8 oz wholemeal plain flour
2 eggs, beaten
1 tbsp wholemeal plain flour,
  for dusting

Great for sharing, this tasty tart is ideal when served either warm or cold, so it can be made ahead and stored in the fridge if you like. Serve with a simple side of assorted salad leaves for an appetizing meat-free lunch.

1. To make the pastry, put the butter and flour in a mixing bowl and season with salt and pepper, if using. Rub the butter into the flour until it resembles fine crumbs. Gradually mix in enough egg to make a soft but not sticky dough.

2. Lightly dust a work surface with wholemeal flour. Knead the pastry gently, then roll it out on the work surface to a little larger than a 25-cm/10-inch loose-bottomed flan tin. Lift the pastry over the rolling pin, ease it into the tin and press it into the sides. Trim the pastry so that it stands a little above the top of the tin to allow for shrinkage, then prick the base with a fork.

3. Cover the tart case with clingfilm and chill in the refrigerator for 15–30 minutes. Meanwhile, preheat the oven to 190°C/375°F/Gas Mark 5.

4. To make the filling, melt the butter in a frying pan over a medium heat. Add the spring onions and cook for 2–3 minutes, or until softened. Add the spinach, turn the heat to high, and cook, stirring, until wilted. Set aside to cool.

5. Place the peas in a small saucepan of boiling water and cook for 2 minutes. Drain, then plunge into iced water and drain again. Crack the eggs into a jug, add the milk, season with salt and pepper, if using, and beat with a fork.

6. Line the tart case with a large sheet of baking paper, add baking beans and place on a baking sheet. Bake for 10 minutes, then remove the paper and beans and bake for 5 minutes more, or until the base of the tart is crisp and dry.

7. Drain any cooking juices from the spring onions and spinach into the eggs. Put the onion mixture in the tart case, add the peas, then sprinkle over the cheese. Whisk the eggs and milk together once more, then pour into the tart case and dot the tomatoes over the top. Bake for 40–50 minutes, or until set and golden. Leave to cool for 20 minutes, then serve.

PER SERVING: *439 Kcals* / *27.1g fat* / *15.6g sat fat* / *35.9g carbs* / *4.9g sugar* / *6.2g fibre* / *16.4g protein* / *0.7g salt*

57

Fresh Pho with Beef

Transport your taste buds across the world and enjoy the enticing fresh and clean flavours of this popular Vietnamese beef and noodle dish, which is good for a flavour-packed lunch with friends.

Serves 4

Prep: 20–25 minutes
Cook: 40 minutes

2 litres/3½ pints beef stock
4-cm/1½-inch piece fresh ginger, sliced
1 star anise
2 cinnamon sticks
5 cloves
75 ml/2½ fl oz fish sauce
1 red chilli, finely sliced
200 g/7 oz rice vermicelli noodles
350 g/12 oz rump or sirloin steak, very finely sliced
100 g/3½ oz mangetout, finely sliced
40 g/1½ oz beansprouts
30 g/1 oz fresh coriander, roughly chopped, to garnish
30 g/1 oz fresh Thai basil, roughly chopped, to garnish
1 tbsp finely sliced red chilli, to garnish

1. Pour the beef stock into a large saucepan. Add the ginger, star anise, cinnamon sticks, cloves, fish sauce and chilli to the saucepan and place the pan over a high heat. Bring the broth to the boil, then reduce the heat and simmer over a low heat, keeping the pan covered with a lid, for 30 minutes.

2. Meanwhile, place the dry noodles into a large bowl and pour boiling water over the top. Leave them for 3–4 minutes, or until they are completely softened. Drain, return to the bowl, cover and set aside.

3. Add the steak strips to the beef broth and allow the steak to poach for 2–3 minutes. Remove the ginger slices, star anise, cinnamon sticks and cloves from the broth with a slotted spoon.

4. Divide the noodles between four deep bowls. Add a handful of raw mangetout and beansprouts, then ladle over the hot broth mixture. Garnish with the coriander, Thai basil and sliced red chilli and serve immediately.

PER SERVING: 366 Kcals / 8.1g fat / 3.3g sat fat / 49.8g carbs / 4.1g sugar / 2.2g fibre / 24.3g protein / 10.1g salt

Chilled Broad Bean Soup

Serves 6

Prep: 30 minutes,
  plus cooling and chilling
Cook: 12 minutes

850 ml/1½ pints vegetable stock
650 g/1 lb 7 oz shelled
   fresh young broad beans
3 tbsp lemon juice
2 tbsp chopped fresh summer savory
salt and pepper, optional
6 tbsp Greek-style natural yogurt, to serve
1 tsp chopped fresh mint, to garnish

Gloriously green, this seasonal chilled summer soup showcases fresh young broad beans when they are at their best.

1. Pour the stock into a large saucepan and bring to the boil. Reduce the heat to a simmer, add the broad beans and cook for about 7 minutes, or until the beans are tender.

2. Remove the pan from the heat and leave to cool slightly. Transfer to a food processor or blender, in batches if necessary, and process until smooth. Push the mixture through a strainer set over a bowl.

3. Stir in the lemon juice and summer savory and season with salt and pepper, if using. Leave to cool completely, then cover with clingfilm and chill in the refrigerator for at least 3 hours.

4. To serve, ladle into chilled bowls or glasses, top each with a tablespoon of yogurt and garnish with mint. Serve immediately.

PER SERVING: *129 Kcals / 2.4g fat / 1.2g sat fat / 14.2g carbs / 2.4g sugar / 7.6g fibre / 10.3g protein / 1.4g salt*

Three Bean & Chia Salad

Serves 4
Prep: 20 minutes
Cook: 9 minutes

200 g/7 oz green beans, halved
200 g/7 oz frozen edamame beans
150 g/5½ oz frozen sweetcorn
400 g/14 oz canned red kidney
    beans, drained and rinsed
2 tbsp chia seeds

Dressing
3 tbsp olive oil
1 tbsp red wine vinegar
1 tsp wholegrain mustard
1 tsp agave syrup
4 tsp finely chopped fresh tarragon
salt and pepper, optional

Choice chia seeds and protein-providing mixed beans add fibre, vitamins and minerals to this super salad, all tossed together in a piquant mustard-tarragon dressing to produce a palate-pleasing energy-boosting lunch.

1. Put the green beans, edamame beans and sweetcorn in a saucepan of boiling water. Bring back to the boil, then simmer for 4 minutes, or until the green beans are just tender. Drain into a colander, rinse with cold water, then drain again and put into a salad bowl.

2. Add the kidney beans and chia seeds to the bowl and toss gently together.

3. To make the dressing, put the oil, vinegar and mustard in a jam jar, then add the agave syrup and tarragon and season with salt and pepper, if using. Screw on the lid and shake well. Drizzle over the salad, toss gently together and serve immediately.

PER SERVING: *302 Kcals / 15.6g fat / 2g sat fat / 24.4g carbs / 4.5g sugar / 11.1g fibre / 13.4g protein / trace salt*

Seabass & Trout Ceviche

Natural, clean flavours come to the fore in this refreshing combination of fresh fish, fruit and vegetables to create the ultimate raw food feast. This is perfect for a nourishing meat-free lunch that is low in fat.

Serves 4

Prep: 30 minutes, plus chilling
Cook: No cooking

2 ruby grapefruits
200 g/7 oz sea bass fillets, skinned, pin-boned
    and cut into cubes
300 g/10½ oz trout fillets, skinned, pin-boned
    and cut into cubes
finely grated zest and juice of 2 limes
1 red chilli, deseeded and finely chopped
½ red onion, finely chopped
1 tbsp virgin olive oil
15 g/½ oz fresh coriander, finely chopped
60 g/2¼ oz mixed baby spinach,
    watercress and rocket salad
salt and pepper, optional

1. Cut the peel and pith away from the grapefruits with a small serrated knife. Hold each one above a bowl and cut between the membranes to release the segments. Squeeze the juice from the membranes into the bowl.

2. Put the sea bass and trout in a china or glass bowl, sprinkle over the lime zest and juice and chilli, then add the red onion, grapefruit segments and juice and oil. Season with salt and pepper, if using, then gently stir so all the fish is evenly coated in the lime juice.

3. Cover and chill in the refrigerator for 1–1½ hours, or until the fish has taken on a cooked appearance. The sea bass should be bright white and the trout should be a paler, even-coloured pink.

4. Add the coriander and stir gently. Arrange the mixed leaf salad on four plates and spoon the ceviche on top, then serve immediately.

PER SERVING: 263 Kcals / 9.7g fat / 1.6g sat fat / 17.8g carbs / 10.1g sugar / 2.9g fibre / 26.7g protein / 0.2g salt

Protein Rice Bowl

Serves 2
Prep: 25 minutes
Cook: 30 minutes

150 g/5½ oz brown rice
2 large eggs
70 g/2½ oz spinach
4 spring onions, finely chopped
1 red chilli, deseeded and finely sliced
½ ripe avocado, sliced
2 tbsp roasted peanuts

Vinaigrette

2 tbsp olive oil
1 tsp Dijon mustard
1 tbsp cider vinegar
juice of ½ a lemon

Brown rice adds important fibre and fresh chilli supplies a bit of heat to this protein-rich vegetarian lunch for two.

1. Place the rice in a large saucepan and cover with twice the volume of water. Bring to the boil and simmer for 25 minutes, or until the rice is tender and the liquid has nearly all disappeared. Continue to simmer for a further few minutes if some liquid remains.

2. Meanwhile, cook your eggs. Bring a small saucepan of water to the boil. Carefully add the eggs to the pan and boil for 7 minutes – the whites will be cooked and the yolks should still be very slightly soft. Drain and pour cold water over the eggs to stop them cooking. When cool enough to handle, tap them on the work surface to crack the shells and peel them. Cut the eggs into quarters.

3. Stir the spinach, half of the spring onions and a little red chilli into the cooked rice.

4. To make the vinaigrette, whisk the olive oil, Dijon mustard, cider vinegar and lemon juice together. Pour the dressing over the warm rice and mix to combine.

5. Divide the rice between two bowls and top each with the remaining spring onions, avocado, remaining red chilli, peanuts and egg quarters.

PER SERVING: 653 Kcals / 33.9g fat / 5.9g sat fat / 71.1g carbs / 4g sugar / 8.7g fibre / 19.1g protein / 0.3g salt

Clams in a Bacon & Leek Broth

Serves 4
Prep: 20–25 minutes
Cook: 20 minutes

1.5 kg/3 lb 5 oz live clams, scrubbed

1 tsp butter

12 streaky bacon rashers,
   roughly chopped

200 g/7 oz leeks, sliced

1 garlic clove, finely chopped

100 ml/3½ fl oz brandy

300 ml/10 fl oz cold water

100 ml/3½ fl oz single cream

25 g/1 oz fresh flat-leaf
   parsley, finely chopped

Natural, fresh clams, bacon and leeks unite in a flavourful creamy broth to make this special lunch for sharing with family or friends. Crusty wholegrain bread to accompany is all you need to complete the meal.

1. Discard any clams with broken shells or any that refuse to close when tapped.

2. Melt the butter in a deep, heavy-based saucepan over a medium heat. Add the bacon and fry, stirring, for 4–5 minutes, or until crisp and golden. Using a slotted spoon, transfer the bacon to a plate lined with kitchen paper.

3. Put the leeks and garlic in the saucepan and cook, stirring regularly, for 5 minutes, or until softened but not browned.

4. Pour in the brandy and leave it to bubble for a minute to burn off the alcohol (brandy in a hot pan can easily flame, so take care). Add the water and stir well. Turn up the heat to medium–high and, when the water starts to boil, toss in the clams. Put on the lid and steam for 5 minutes, or until the clams have opened.

5. Take the saucepan off the heat. Discard any clams that remain closed. Stir in the bacon and cream. Stir in the parsley and serve in bowls, with a large empty bowl to collect the clam shells.

PER SERVING: 350 Kcals / 42.6g fat / 17.3g sat fat / 10.6g carbs / 2g sugar / 1.1g fibre / 57.9g protein / 7g salt

Flatbread Pizza with Courgette Ribbons

Quinoa flour adds extra nutrients and appeal to these energy-packed home-made flatbread pizzas, topped with vibrant vegetables and drizzled with garlic oil. Delicious served freshly baked and warm from the oven.

Serves 2
Prep: 30 minutes
Cook: 7–10 minutes

50 g/1¾ oz crème fraîche
150 g/5½ oz courgettes, shredded into ribbons
   using a vegetable peeler
55 g/2 oz cherry tomatoes, quartered
50 g/1¾ oz ricotta cheese
1 garlic clove, crushed
2 tbsp olive oil

Pizza bases
100 g/3½ oz wholemeal plain flour
50 g/1¾ oz quinoa flour
¾ tsp bicarbonate of soda
1 tbsp olive oil
2 tbsp warm water
1 tbsp wholemeal plain flour, for dusting
salt, optional

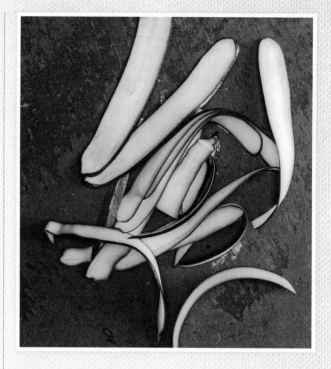

1. Preheat the oven to 200°C/400°F/Gas Mark 6. To make the pizza bases, put the flours and bicarbonate of soda in a mixing bowl, season with salt, if using, and stir. Add the oil, then gradually mix in enough of the warm water to make a soft but not sticky dough.

2. Lightly dust a work surface with flour. Knead the dough on the surface for 2 minutes, or until the dough is smooth and slightly elastic.

3. Put two large, flat baking sheets in the oven to get hot.

4. Divide the dough into two pieces. Roll out each piece to a circle about 5 mm/¼ inch thick. Remove the hot baking sheets from the oven and, working quickly, lay the dough on top. Spread the crème fraîche over the dough, then sprinkle with the courgettes and tomatoes. Blob the ricotta cheese in small dollops on top.

5. Bake the pizzas for 7–10 minutes, or until the crust is crispy and slightly puffed up, and the ricotta has started to turn golden.

6. Mix the garlic and oil together in a jug, and drizzle over the pizzas. Serve immediately.

PER SERVING: 592 Kcals / 34.4g fat / 10.7g sat fat / 60g carbs / 3.3g sugar / 8.7g fibre / 15.2g protein / 1.2g salt

Asparagus with Hot-smoked Salmon & Poached Egg

Serves 2

Prep: 25 minutes, plus chilling
Cook: 26–28 minutes

50 g/1¾ oz unsalted butter, softened
finely grated zest of ½ lemon
½ tsp lemon juice
sprig of fresh dill, roughly chopped
400 g/14 oz hot-smoked salmon
10 asparagus spears,
   woody stems removed
2 large eggs
salt and pepper, optional

Rich in important omega-3 fatty acids, flakes of hot-smoked salmon are served with antioxidant-rich fresh asparagus spears and good-for-you poached eggs in this scrumptiously satisfying lunch for two to share.

1. Preheat the oven to 180°C/350°F/Gas Mark 4. Put the butter, lemon zest and juice and dill in a small bowl, season with salt and pepper, if using, and mix. Pat the butter into a rough square with the back of a spoon, wrap it in clingfilm and chill in the refrigerator while you make the rest of the dish.

2. Wrap the hot-smoked salmon in kitchen foil and bake in the preheated oven for 15 minutes. Flake the fish into bite-sized pieces and keep warm.

3. Cook the asparagus in a small saucepan of boiling water for 2 minutes. Drain and run under a cold tap briefly to stop the cooking process, then set aside.

4. Heat a second wide saucepan of water until it is almost at simmering point. Crack one egg into a cup, then stir the water to make a whirlpool. As the whirlpool slows almost to a stop, gently slip the egg into its centre. Cook for 2–3 minutes, then remove with a slotted spoon. Repeat with the second egg.

5. Put five asparagus spears on each of two plates, top with half the flaked salmon, then balance a poached egg on top and crown with half of the lemon butter. The heat from the egg should melt the butter into a scrumptious lemon-herb sauce. Serve immediately.

PER SERVING: *648 Kcals / 45.6g fat / 19.4g sat fat / 3.9g carbs / 1.8g sugar / 1.8g fibre / 56.2g protein / 7.6g salt*

Rainbow Nori Rolls

Brightly-coloured vegetables, high in antioxidants, provide the nutritious filling for these nourishing sushi-style nori rolls. They are the ideal choice for a special lunch with a small gathering of friends.

Serves 4

Prep: 30–35 minutes, plus cooling and chilling
Cook: 27–30 minutes

175 g/6 oz sushi rice
750 ml/1¼ pints cold water
2 tbsp mirin
1 tbsp light olive oil
100 g/3½ oz asparagus tips
4 sheets nori
100 g/3½ oz sliced sushi ginger, drained
25 g/1 oz kale, cut into thin strips
1 small red pepper, halved, deseeded and cut into thin strips
1 small yellow pepper, halved, deseeded and cut into thin strips
100 g/3½ oz carrots, cut into matchstick strips
100 g/3½ oz cooked beetroot in natural juices,
   drained and cut into matchstick strips
2 tbsp tamari
2 tbsp Chinese rice wine
salt, optional

1. Put the rice and water, with a little salt if using, into a saucepan and bring to the boil, stirring occasionally. Reduce the heat and gently simmer for 18–20 minutes, until the rice is soft and has absorbed all the water. Stir occasionally towards the end of cooking so that the rice doesn't stick to the base of the pan. Remove from the heat and stir in the mirin. Leave to cool for 10 minutes.

2. Heat the oil in a frying pan, add the asparagus and fry over a medium heat for 3–4 minutes, until just soft, then set aside.

3. Separate the nori sheets and place one on a piece of clingfilm set on top of a bamboo sushi mat. Thinly spread one quarter of the warm rice over the top to cover the nori sheet completely.

4. Arrange one quarter of the ginger in an overlapping line a little up from one edge of the nori. Arrange one quarter of the asparagus and kale next to it, then one quarter of the red pepper and yellow pepper, then one quarter of the carrot and beetroot, leaving a border of rice about 2 cm/¾ inch wide.

5. Using the clingfilm and sushi mat, tightly roll the nori around the vegetables. Remove the bamboo mat, then twist the ends of the clingfilm and place the roll on a tray. Repeat to make three more nori rolls, then chill for 1 hour, or longer if preferred.

6. To serve, mix the tamari and rice wine together, then spoon into four small dipping bowls and set the bowls on serving plates. Unwrap each nori roll and cut into five thick slices. Arrange, cut-side up, on the serving plates and serve immediately.

PER SERVING: *280 Kcals / 4.1g fat / 0.6g sat fat / 50.9g carbs / 7.7g sugar / 5.7g fibre / 6.7g protein / 3.4g salt*

Turkey Wraps with Avocado Salsa

Wraps are meant for sharing, so these feel-good eats give a great energy boost at lunchtime and are just right for a wholesome weekend of eating al fresco with family or friends. The fun is in the assembling!

Serves 4

Prep: 30 minutes, plus marinating
Cook: 12 minutes

4 thin turkey breast escalopes, 350 g/12 oz total weight
1 tbsp olive oil, for brushing
4 cos lettuce leaves, thick stems removed
    and leaves sliced into ribbons
4 corn tortillas, warmed
3 tbsp soured cream

Marinade

juice of 2 oranges
1 tsp cumin seeds, lightly crushed
½ tsp dried red chilli flakes
4 tbsp olive oil
salt and pepper, optional

Salsa

2 avocados, diced
1 small red onion, diced
2 tomatoes, deseeded and diced
2 tbsp chopped fresh coriander
juice of 1 lime

1. Slice the turkey into 4 x 6-cm/1½ x 2½-inch strips. Place in a shallow dish.

2. To make the marinade, whisk together all the marinade ingredients and season with salt and pepper, if using. Pour over the turkey, cover and marinate in the refrigerator for at least 4 hours. Remove at least 30 minutes before cooking to bring to room temperature.

3. To make the salsa, mix all the ingredients in a bowl.

4. Preheat the grill to very high. Drain the turkey, discarding the marinade. Thread the strips in a concertina-style onto metal skewers (or use wooden skewers with aluminium foil wrapped around the ends so that they don't burn) and brush with oil. Place the skewers on a rack in the grill pan and cook under the preheated grill for about 5 minutes on each side, or until the turkey is cooked through, with no pink in the centre and starting to brown at the edges. Remove the turkey from the skewers, set aside and keep warm.

5. Divide the lettuce between the warmed tortillas and arrange the turkey on top. Add a little soured cream and salsa. Roll the bottoms and sides of the tortillas over the filling and serve immediately.

PER SERVING: *487 Kcals / 26g fat / 5g sat fat / 37.2g carbs / 6.2g sugar / 9.6g fibre / 28.5g protein / 0.6g salt*

Spicy Rice with Chicken & Pomegranate

Spice up your lunch with this very tempting chicken and rice dish, finished with fleshy pink pomegranate seeds, which pack a powerful nutrient punch, plus vivid green antioxidant-rich fresh herbs.

Serves 4

Prep: 25 minutes, plus cooling
Cook: 45–50 minutes

4 large chicken thighs
2 tsp Chinese five spice
2 tbsp olive oil
2 red onions, finely sliced
2 garlic cloves, finely sliced
5 cardamom pods, crushed
2 star anise
250 g/9 oz brown rice
750 ml/1¼ pints vegetable stock
25 g/1 oz fresh mint, roughly chopped
25 g/1 oz fresh flat-leaf parsley, roughly chopped
seeds of 1 small pomegranate
4 tbsp toasted almonds
grated zest and juice of 1 lemon
salt and pepper, optional

1. Preheat the oven to 200°C/400°F/Gas Mark 6. Place the chicken thighs on a baking tray and sprinkle over the Chinese five spice. Drizzle over 1 tablespoon of olive oil and roast in the preheated oven for 20 minutes, or until the juices run clear when the thickest part of the meat is pierced and no traces of pink remain in the centre. Remove from the oven and set aside to cool.

2. Meanwhile, heat the remaining tablespoon of olive oil in a large saucepan over a medium–low heat. Add the onion and gently fry for 10–12 minutes, or until soft and starting to caramelize. Stir in the garlic, cardamom pods and star anise and cook for a further minute. Add the rice and stir well.

3. Pour in the stock and bring the pan to the boil. Cover and simmer gently for 25–30 minutes, or until all the stock has been absorbed and the rice is tender.

PER SERVING: *675 Kcals / 33.9g fat / 7.7g sat fat / 64.2g carbs / 7.8g sugar / 6.2g fibre / 30.3g protein / 2.2g salt*

4. Once the chicken is cool enough to handle, remove the meat from the bones and finely slice. Add to the rice mixture, with any remaining juices, and season with salt and pepper, if using.

5. Stir in half of the mint and parsley. Top with the remaining herbs, pomegranate seeds, toasted almonds, lemon juice and zest and serve immediately.

No-crust Squash & Goat's Cheese Quiche

Try your hand at making your own wholemeal shortcrust pastry with this fabulous energy-fuelled quiche, that can be served warm or cold. Serve with a salad of mixed lettuce leaves and peppery rocket.

Serves 4

Prep: 35 minutes, plus chilling and cooling
Cook: 1 hour 20 minutes

400 g/14 oz butternut squash flesh, diced
1 tbsp olive oil
200 g/7 oz chorizo, cut into small, irregular chunks
3 eggs
100 ml/3½ fl oz crème fraîche
2 tbsp fresh thyme leaves
100 g/3½ oz semi-hard goat's cheese
salt and pepper, optional

Pastry

50 g/1¾ oz cold butter, diced
100 g/3½ oz wholemeal plain flour
2 tbsp cold water
2 tbsp wholemeal plain flour, for dusting

1. Preheat the oven to 190°C/375°F/Gas Mark 5. To make the pastry, put the butter in a bowl, add the flour and season with salt and pepper, if using. Rub the butter into the flour until it resembles breadcrumbs. Alternatively, process it in a food processor. Gradually mix in enough of the water to make a soft but not sticky dough.

2. Lightly dust a work surface with flour. Pat the dough into a disc, then wrap it in clingfilm. Chill in the refrigerator for at least 30 minutes.

3. Meanwhile, to make the filling, put the butternut squash and oil in a large roasting tin, season with salt and pepper, if using, and toss well. Roast in the preheated oven for 15 minutes, then stir and add the chorizo. Roast for 15 minutes more, or until the squash is crisp and tender, and the chorizo is crisp. Set aside to cool.

4. Dust the work surface with more flour. Knead the pastry gently, then roll it out to a circle just under 23 cm/9 inches in diameter. Place on a baking sheet and prick all over with a fork. Bake for 20 minutes. Remove from the oven and, using the base of a 20-cm/8-inch loose-bottomed tart tin as a template, cut a circle in the pastry. Set aside to cool.

5. Meanwhile, crack the eggs into a large bowl and lightly beat with a fork. Stir in the crème fraîche and thyme and season with pepper, if using.

6. Line the 20-cm/8-inch tart tin with baking paper. Carefully place your cooled pastry circle in the tin, then scatter with the chorizo and butternut squash. Pour over the egg mixture, then crumble the goat's cheese on top. Reduce the oven temperature to 160°C/325°F/Gas Mark 3. Bake the quiche for 30 minutes, or until the egg in the centre is set. Serve warm or cold.

PER SERVING: *724 Kcals / 54.7g fat / 26.2g sat fat / 34.7g carbs / 3.9g sugar / 5.3g fibre / 26.8g protein / 2.5g salt*

Seared Beef Salad

Lightly seared succulent sirloin steaks add an important protein and iron boost to this super salad, made even more nutritious by the colourful on-trend addition of bright red superfood goji berries.

Serves 4

Prep: 25 minutes
Cook: 6–10 minutes, plus resting

½ iceberg lettuce, leaves separated and torn into bite-sized pieces
200 g/7 oz radishes, thinly sliced
4 shallots, thinly sliced
85 g/3 oz kale, shredded
2 tbsp dried goji berries
25 g/1 oz fresh mint, roughly chopped
25 g/1 oz fresh coriander, roughly chopped
2 x 250 g/9 oz sirloin steaks, visible fat removed
4 tbsp sunflower oil
juice of 1 lime
1 tbsp soy sauce
salt and pepper, optional

1. Put the lettuce, radishes and shallots in a serving bowl. Sprinkle over the kale, goji berries, mint and coriander, then toss gently together.

2. Preheat a ridged griddle pan over a high heat. Brush the steaks with 1 tablespoon of oil, then sprinkle with salt and pepper, if using. Cook in the hot pan for 2 minutes on each side for medium–rare, 3 minutes for medium or 4 minutes for well done. Transfer the steaks to a plate and leave to rest for a few minutes.

3. Meanwhile, put the lime juice, soy sauce and remaining 3 tablespoons of oil in a jam jar, screw on the lid and shake well. Drizzle over the salad, then toss together.

4. Divide the salad between four bowls. Thinly slice the steak and arrange it over the top, then serve immediately.

PER SERVING: 353 Kcals / 19.1g fat / 3.2g sat fat / 14.8g carbs / 5.7g sugar / 3.7g fibre / 31.3g protein / 0.8g salt

Prawn-filled Sweet Jacket Potatoes

<u>Serves 4</u>
Prep: 25 minutes, plus chilling
Cook: 1 hour

4 x 250 g/9 oz sweet potatoes,
    scrubbed and pricked with a fork
85 g/3 oz frozen sweetcorn
125 g/4½ oz plum
    tomatoes, cut into cubes
4 spring onions, finely chopped
1 mango, cut into cubes
15 g/½ oz fresh coriander,
    finely chopped
1 red chilli, deseeded and
    finely chopped, optional
300 g/10½ oz cooked
    and peeled prawns
finely grated zest and juice of 1 lime
300 g/10½ oz low-fat cottage cheese
salt and pepper, optional

Deliciously good for you, adults and children alike will love these zesty prawn and mango salsa-crammed sweet jacket potatoes.

1. Preheat the oven to 200°C/400°F/ Gas Mark 6. Put the sweet potatoes on a baking tray and bake in the preheated for 1 hour, or until they feel soft when gently squeezed.

2. Meanwhile, bring a saucepan of water to the boil, add the frozen sweetcorn and cook for 3 minutes, or until tender. Drain into a sieve, then rinse under cold running water.

3. Put the tomatoes, spring onions and mango in a bowl, then stir in the coriander, red chilli, if using, and sweetcorn. Season with salt and pepper, if using. Cover and chill in the refrigerator.

4. Put the prawns and lime zest and juice in another bowl and season with salt and pepper, if using. Cover and chill in the refrigerator.

5. Put the potatoes on a serving plate, slit them in half, then open them out. Top with spoonfuls of the cottage cheese, then fill with the salsa and prawns.

PER SERVING: *408 Kcals / 2.4g fat / 0.7g sat fat / 71.9g carbs / 23.7g sugar / 8g fibre / 24.1g protein / 1.9g salt*

Good-for-you
Cobb Salad

As energy levels start to flag, this rich-in-protein layered salad is the perfect choice for those in need of a sustaining and tasty salad at lunchtime. For more mighty appetites, serve with crusty fresh wholemeal bread alongside.

Serves 2
Prep: 25 minutes
Cook: 50 minutes

Cobb salad
100 g/3½ oz wild rice
2 large eggs
1 tbsp olive oil, for frying
2 rashers bacon, cut into 2-cm/¾-inch pieces
1 small avocado, sliced
2 tomatoes, cut into quarters
30 g/1 oz watercress
2 tbsp finely snipped fresh chives, to garnish

Dressing
2 tbsp cider vinegar
1 tbsp lemon juice
2 tsp Dijon mustard
1 garlic clove, crushed
2 tbsp olive oil

1. To make the Cobb salad, put the wild rice in a small saucepan with 350 ml/12 fl oz of cold water and place over a high heat. Bring the pan to the boil and then reduce the heat to low. Simmer the rice for 25 minutes, or until tender. Drain away any excess water and set aside.

2. To make the dressing, place the vinegar, lemon juice, mustard, crushed garlic and olive oil in a jam jar or small bowl. Whisk well until the dressing is thoroughly combined and set aside.

3. Bring another small saucepan of water to boiling point and gently add the eggs to the pan. Simmer the eggs for 10 minutes. Remove the eggs from the pan and run them under cold water to stop the cooking process. Peel away the egg shells and cut into quarters. Set the egg quarters aside.

PER SERVING: 705 Kcals / 49.3g fat / 10.2g sat fat / 48.6g carbs / 4g sugar / 9.2g fibre / 20.9g protein / 0.8g salt

4. Add the olive oil to a small saucepan and place over a high heat. Fry the bacon pieces for 4–5 minutes, stirring continuously, or until the bacon is crispy and golden. Set aside.

5. Layer the rice, bacon pieces, avocado, tomatoes, quartered eggs and watercress between two bowls. Garnish with the chives and drizzle over the dressing. Serve immediately.

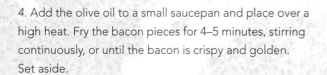

Vietnamese Tofu & Noodle Salad

Serves 4

Prep: 30 minutes, plus
  marinating and cooling
Cook: 12 minutes

400 g/14 oz firm chilled tofu,
  drained and cut into 8 slices
115 g/4 oz buckwheat soba noodles
200 g/7 oz frozen edamame beans
1 carrot, cut into matchstick strips
85 g/3 oz mangetout, cut
  into matchstick strips
115 g/4 oz rainbow chard,
  stems cut into matchstick strips,
  leaves thinly shredded
15 g/½ oz fresh coriander,
  roughly chopped

Marinade

2 tbsp soy sauce
2 tbsp sesame seeds
1 red chilli, deseeded and
  finely chopped, optional
4-cm/1½-inch piece fresh
  ginger, finely chopped

Dressing

4 tbsp virgin rapeseed oil
juice of ½ lemon
1 tbsp sweet chilli dipping sauce

This marvellous meat-free salad combines beneficial buckwheat soba noodles with marinated grilled tofu, nutritious mixed vegetables and protein-dense edamame beans, all drizzled with a simple chilli-spiced salad dressing to serve.

1. Line the base of the grill pan with foil. Arrange the tofu on the grill pan in a single layer and fold up the edges of the foil to make a dish.

2. To make the marinade, mix together the soy sauce, sesame seeds, chilli, if using, and half of the ginger in a small bowl. Spoon this over the tofu, then leave to marinate for 10 minutes.

3. Bring a large saucepan of water to the boil, add the noodles and frozen edamame beans and cook for 3–4 minutes, or until just tender. Drain into a sieve, then rinse under cold running water.

4. Put the carrot, mangetout, rainbow chard stems and leaves and coriander in a large salad bowl. Add the noodles and edamame beans and gently toss.

5. To make the dressing, put the oil, lemon juice, sweet chilli dipping sauce and remaining ginger in a bowl and whisk with a fork. Pour over the salad and gently toss.

6. Preheat the grill to medium–high. Turn the tofu over in the marinade, then grill for 2 minutes on each side, or until browned. Leave to cool for a few minutes, then cut into cubes and sprinkle over the salad with any remaining marinade and serve.

PER SERVING: *412 Kcals / 22.8g fat / 2.1g sat fat / 33.2g carbs / 6g sugar / 4.9g fibre / 19.9g protein / 2.1g salt*

Avocado, Bacon & Chilli Frittata

Serves 4
Prep: 20–25 minutes
Cook: 12–16 minutes

1 tbsp vegetable oil

8 streaky bacon rashers, roughly chopped

6 eggs, beaten

3 tbsp double cream

2 large avocados, sliced

1 red chilli, deseeded and thinly sliced

½ lime

salt and pepper, optional

Bursting with nourishing nutrients, ripe avocados add appealing flavour, colour and creamy texture to this pan-fried frittata.

1. Preheat the grill to medium. Heat the oil in a 20-cm/8-inch ovenproof frying pan over a medium heat. Add the bacon and fry, stirring, for 4–5 minutes, or until crisp and golden. Using a slotted spoon, transfer to a plate lined with kitchen paper. Remove the pan from the heat.

2. Pour the eggs into a bowl, add the cream and season with salt and pepper, if using, then beat. Return the pan to the heat. When it is hot, pour in the egg mixture and cook for 1–2 minutes, without stirring. Sprinkle the bacon and avocado on top and cook for a further 2–3 minutes, or until the frittata is almost set and the underside is golden brown.

3. Place the frittata under the grill and cook for 3–4 minutes, or until the top is golden brown and the egg is set. Scatter over the chilli and squeeze over the lime juice. Cut into wedges and serve.

PER SERVING: *445 Kcals / 53.4g fat / 16.6g sat fat / 10.9g carbs / 1.6g sugar / 6.9g fibre / 43.9g protein / 4.3g salt*

Super-charged
Snacks & Sides

Fig & Oat Bites

The goodness of wholegrain oats paired with fibre-rich dried figs creates these scrumptious nuggets of goodness that contain no added sugar or salt. A sprinkling of chia seeds and spices boosts their feel-good factor further.

Makes 25
Prep: 20–25 minutes, plus cooling
Cook: 20 minutes

450 g/1 lb soft dried figs
3 tbsp coconut oil, at room temperature
½ tsp ground ginger
½ tsp ground cinnamon
juice of 1 large orange
200 g/7 oz rolled oats
1 tbsp chia seeds

1. Preheat the oven to 180°C/350°F/Gas Mark 4. Line a 23-cm/9-inch square baking tin with baking paper.

2. Place the dried figs, coconut oil, ginger and cinnamon into a food processor and pulse until roughly chopped. Add the orange juice and oats and pulse again until the mixture just comes together. If a little dry, add a touch more orange juice; if a little wet, stir through a few more oats. Add the chia seeds and pulse again very briefly.

3. Spoon the mixture into the prepared baking tin. Use the back of a greased spatula to push the mixture to the corners and spread it evenly.

4. Bake in the preheated oven for 20 minutes. Remove from the oven and, using a sharp knife, cut into 25 small squares. Leave to cool completely on a wire rack and then serve.

PER SQUARE: *93 Kcals / 2.4g fat / 1.5g sat fat / 17.5g carbs / 9g sugar / 2.8g fibre / 1.7g protein / trace salt*

Honey & Spice Snacking Nuts

Serves 6
Prep: 15–20 minutes
Cook: 10 minutes

75 g/2¾ oz Brazil nuts
50 g/1¾ oz pecan nuts
50 g/1¾ oz cashew nuts
25 g/1 oz pumpkin seeds
1 tbsp sunflower oil
1½ tbsp runny honey
½ tsp ground cinnamon
½ tsp ground mixed spice
½ tsp ground black pepper
½ tsp sweet paprika
¼ tsp salt

Gluten and dairy free, these sensational spiced nuts are quick and easy to make and great for a healthy snack.

1. Line a baking tray with baking paper. Preheat the oven to 140°C/275°F/Gas Mark 1.

2. Combine all the ingredients in a bowl, except for half a tablespoon of the honey, and then spread out onto the prepared baking tray.

3. Place onto the middle shelf of the oven and cook for 10 minutes. Remove from the oven and drizzle the remaining honey over the nuts. Leave to cool, then serve. These snacking nuts can be stored in an airtight container for up to a week.

PER SERVING: *247 Kcals / 22.3g fat / 3.6g sat fat / 10.5g carbs / 5.5g sugar / 2.5g fibre / 5.4g protein / 0.2g salt*

Roasted Kale Crisps

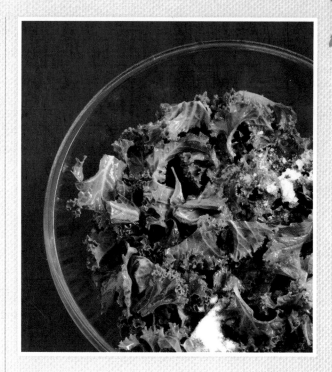

Kale boasts a multitude of nourishing nutrients and these roasted kale crisps are perfect for munching on with a gathering of friends. They make a great alternative to potato crisps or tortilla chips.

Serves 4
Prep: 20 minutes
Cook: 10–12 minutes

250 g/9 oz kale
2 tbsp olive oil
2 pinches of sugar
2 pinches of sea salt
2 tbsp toasted flaked almonds, to garnish

1. Preheat the oven to 150°C/300°F/Gas Mark 2. Remove the thick stems and central rib from the kale (leaving about 125 g/4½ oz trimmed leaves). Rinse and dry very thoroughly with kitchen paper. Tear into bite-sized pieces and place in a bowl with the oil and sugar, then toss well.

2. Spread about half the leaves in a single layer in a large roasting tin, spaced well apart. Sprinkle with a pinch of sea salt and roast on the bottom rack of the preheated oven for 4 minutes.

3. Stir the leaves, then turn the tray so the back is at the front. Roast for a further 1–2 minutes, until the leaves are crisp and very slightly browned at the edges. Repeat with the remaining leaves and sea salt. Sprinkle the kale crisps with the flaked almonds and serve immediately.

PER SERVING: *122 Kcals / 9.6g fat / 1.1g sat fat / 8.1g carbs / 1.2g sugar / 1.7g fibre / 3g protein / 0.4g salt*

Frozen Yogurt Berries

Serves 4

Prep: 20–25 minutes, plus freezing
Cook: No cooking

225 g/8 oz low-fat Greek-style natural yogurt
1 tbsp runny honey
¼ tsp vanilla extract
115 g/4 oz blueberries
125 g/4½ oz raspberries

These berries are perfect for a healthy, quick fix snack when you've got a sweet craving.

1. Line three baking sheets or trays with non-stick baking paper, checking first that they will fit into your freezer.

2. Place the yogurt, honey and vanilla extract in a medium-sized bowl and stir together. Drop a few blueberries into the yogurt, then use two forks to coat the berries in a thin layer of yogurt. Lift out, one berry at a time, draining off the excess yogurt, and transfer to one of the lined trays.

3. Continue dipping and coating until all the blueberries are on the tray. Repeat with the raspberries. Freeze, uncovered, for 2–3 hours, until frozen solid.

4. Lift the berries from the trays and pack into polythene bags or lidded plastic containers. Seal and freeze for up to 1 month.

5. Remove as many as you need from the freezer and leave to thaw for 10 minutes before serving so that the fruit can soften slightly.

Smoky Paprika Roasted Chickpeas

Serves 4

Prep: 15–20 minutes, plus cooling
Cook: 18–24 minutes

2 tbsp olive oil
1 tsp cumin seeds, roughly crushed
1 tsp smoked mild paprika
¼ tsp ground allspice
¼ tsp ground cinnamon
½ tsp sea salt
800 g/1 lb 12 oz canned chickpeas in water, drained and rinsed
2 tbsp date syrup

1. Preheat the oven to 200°C/400°F/Gas Mark 6. Add the oil to a roasting tin and place in the oven to heat for 3–4 minutes.

2. Add the cumin seeds, paprika, allspice, cinnamon and salt to a small bowl, and mix together well.

3. Add the chickpeas to the roasting tin, drizzle over the date syrup, sprinkle with the spice mix and stir together. Roast in the preheated oven for 15–20 minutes, stirring once, until brown and crunchy.

4. Spoon into a bowl and leave to cool before eating. Store any leftovers in a plastic container or preserving jar in the refrigerator for up to 1 week.

This is a quick and economical snack to make and perfect for having on the go. For an extra smoky flavour, drizzle over some tahini when adding the date syrup.

PER SERVING: 243 Kcals / 9.3g fat / 1.2g sat fat / 29.9g carbs / 12.3g sugar / 7.8g fibre / 8.9g protein / 0.8g salt

Date Power Balls

Makes 20
Prep: 30–35 minutes
Cook: No cooking

85 g/3 oz 70% plain chocolate
40 g/1½ oz sunflower seeds
40 g/1½ oz linseeds
40 g/1½ oz sesame seeds
100 g/3½ oz Brazil nuts,
    roughly chopped
140 g/5 oz Medjool dates, stoned
40 g/1½ oz goji berries
1 tsp ground cinnamon
1 tbsp maca
40 g/1½ oz unsweetened
    desiccated coconut
6 tbsp maple syrup

These fibre-filled, moreish Medjool date power balls are guaranteed to boost your energy levels at any time of the day. These can be made ahead and stored in the refrigerator for a top-pick snappy snack.

1. Break 55 g/2 oz chocolate into pieces and reserve the rest. Put the sunflower seeds, linseeds, sesame seeds, Brazil nuts and chocolate pieces in a food processor and process until finely ground, scraping down the sides of the processor once or twice.

2. Add the dates, goji berries, cinnamon, maca and 25 g/1 oz coconut, then spoon in the maple syrup. Process until you have a coarse paste.

3. Using a measuring spoon, scoop out tablespoons of the mixture onto a plate, then adjust the sizes of the mounds to make 20. Roll them into balls.

4. Put the remaining coconut on one plate and finely grate the remaining chocolate onto another plate. Roll half of the balls in the coconut and the rest in the chocolate. Pack into an airtight container and store in the fridge for up to 3 days.

Rosemary, Sea Salt & Sesame Popcorn

The perfect power snack, fresh rosemary adds a subtle herby flavour to this sensational seeded popcorn, best enjoyed freshly popped and warm. It's great for snacking on when you fancy something savoury and sustaining.

Serves 4

Prep: 10–15 minutes
Cook: 6–8 minutes

40 g/1½ oz sesame seeds
2 tbsp olive oil
2 rosemary stems, torn into large pieces
200 g/7 oz popping corn
1 tsp sea salt
2 tbsp balsamic vinegar

1. Add the sesame seeds to a large frying pan with 1 teaspoon of the oil. Cover and cook over a medium heat for 2–3 minutes, shaking the pan from time to time, until the seeds are toasted golden brown and beginning to pop. Scoop out of the pan into a bowl and wipe out the pan with a piece of kitchen paper.

2. Add the remaining oil and the rosemary to the pan and heat gently, shaking the pan to release the rosemary's oil. Add the corn, cover with the lid and cook over a medium heat for 3–4 minutes, shaking the pan, until all the popcorn has popped.

3. Remove from the heat and sprinkle with the toasted sesame seeds and season with the salt and vinegar, then tip into a serving bowl, discarding the rosemary just before eating.

PER SERVING: *379 Kcals / 25.2g fat / 3.2g sat fat / 30g carbs / 1.6g sugar / 6.6g fibre / 6.4g protein / 1.5g salt*

Butternut Wedges with Sage & Pumpkin Seeds

Serves 3
Prep: 20 minutes
Cook: 35 minutes

1 large butternut squash
1 tbsp olive oil
½ tsp chilli powder
12 fresh sage leaves, finely chopped
50 g/1¾ oz pumpkin seeds
salt and pepper, optional

1. Preheat the oven to 200°C/400°F/Gas Mark 6. Prepare the butternut squash by washing any excess dirt from the skin and slicing off the very top and very bottom.

2. Using a sharp knife and a steady hand, cut the squash into six long wedges. Scoop out any seeds and discard. Place the wedges on a baking tray. Brush with half of the olive oil and sprinkle with the chilli powder. Roast in the preheated oven for 25 minutes.

3. Remove from the oven and brush with the remaining olive oil. Sprinkle over the sage and pumpkin seeds. Season with salt and pepper, if using, and return the wedges to the oven for a further 10 minutes. Serve immediately, garnished with extra pepper, if using.

Once roasted, cut the squash into smaller cubes and toss with toasted couscous for a simple lunch. The edible skin has been kept on in this recipe but you can peel it off if that is your preference.

PER SERVING: 259 Kcals / 13.3g fat / 2.1g sat fat / 33.9g carbs / 6.1g sugar / 7.2g fibre / 7.8g protein / trace salt

Spiced Carrot Mash

Serves 4

Prep: 20 minutes, plus cooling
Cook: 30–35 minutes

1.25 kg/2 lb 12 oz carrots, cut in half lengthways
1 small bulb of garlic, cloves peeled
1 tsp ground turmeric
1 tsp ground coriander
1 tsp ground cumin
2 tbsp olive oil
salt and pepper, optional
2 tsp black onion seeds, to garnish
1 tbsp roughly chopped fresh flat-leaf parsley, to garnish, optional

1. Preheat the oven to 200°C/400°F/Gas Mark 6.

2. Place the carrots, garlic cloves, turmeric, coriander and cumin in a large roasting tin. Drizzle over the olive oil and stir well, until the carrots are coated thoroughly. Season with salt and pepper, if using.

3. Roast in the preheated oven for 30–35 minutes, or until soft. Turn once, about halfway through, to ensure even cooking.

4. Remove from the oven and leave to cool slightly. Firmly mash the carrot mixture until you have a soft consistency, adding a touch of hot water if needed. Season again to taste, if desired.

5. Serve immediately in a warmed serving dish, garnished with black onion seeds and parsley, if desired.

This is a versatile side dish, suitable for roasts, tarts or salads. Try experimenting with other roast vegetables, such as swede, sweet potato or parsnip, for a slightly different variation.

PER SERVING: 205 Kcals / 7.8g fat / 1g sat fat / 33.3g carbs / 14.9g sugar / 9.3g fibre / 3.6g protein / 0.5g salt

Sweet Potato Falafels

Oven roasting these tasty sesame-coated sweet potato and chickpea falafels, rather than frying them, helps to keep their fat content down and creates an energy-boosting vegetarian snack, ideal for sharing. Enjoy them either hot or cold.

Makes 16

Prep: 30–35 minutes, plus chilling
Cook: 35–40 minutes

2 sweet potatoes (about 550 g/1 lb 4 oz), cut into chunks
3 tsp ground cumin
1 tsp ground coriander
1 tsp ground turmeric
1 tbsp olive oil, for roasting
400 g/14 oz canned chickpeas, drained and rinsed
75 g/2¾ oz chickpea flour
25 g/1 oz fresh flat-leaf parsley, leaves picked
25 g/1 oz fresh coriander, leaves picked
1 tsp salt
100 g/3½ oz sesame seeds
2 tbsp olive oil, for drizzling
100 g/3½ oz natural yogurt, to serve

1. Preheat the oven to 200°C/400°F/Gas Mark 6. Place the sweet potato chunks in a roasting tray. Sprinkle over 2 teaspoons of the cumin and all of the ground coriander and turmeric. Pour over the olive oil and mix well so the sweet potatoes are coated in the spice paste. Make sure the chunks are spread in an even layer and roast in the preheated oven for 20 minutes.

2. Remove the sweet potatoes from the oven and transfer them to a food processor. Add the chickpeas, chickpea flour, parsley, coriander, salt and the remaining teaspoon of cumin. Blitz to a paste. Don't overwork the mixture – stop as soon as you have a paste. Transfer the mixture to a refrigerator and leave to chill for 15–20 minutes.

PER FALAFEL: *132 Kcals / 6.6g fat / 1g sat fat / 14.8g carbs / 3g sugar / 3.4g fibre / 3.8g protein / 0.4g salt*

3. Preheat the oven again to 180°C/350°F/Gas Mark 4. Shape the cooled chickpea mixture into 16 golf-ball-sized pieces. Roll each ball in sesame seeds, drizzle with 1 tablespoon of the olive oil and roast in the preheated oven for 15–20 minutes, turning the falafels over halfway through. At the end of the cooking time, the sesame seeds should be golden.

4. Drizzle the hot falafels with the remaining olive oil and serve with the yogurt. Serve immediately or store in the refrigerator and eat chilled within 24 hours.

Cranberry & Red Cabbage Slaw

Quick and easy to assemble, this colourful slaw is a refreshing combination of raw vegetables and fruit, boosted with dried cranberries, chopped walnuts and chia seeds, to create a satisfying side for vegetarians and vegans.

Serves 4
Prep: 20 minutes, plus optional chilling
Cook: 2–3 minutes

150 g/5½ oz red cabbage, thinly shredded
1 carrot, coarsely grated
140 g/5 oz cauliflower, cut into florets
1 red-skinned dessert apple, quartered, cored and very thinly sliced
40 g/1½ oz dried cranberries
50 g/1¾ oz alfalfa and sango radish shoots

Dressing
50 g/1¾ oz walnuts, roughly chopped
juice of 1 orange
4 tbsp virgin olive oil
2 tbsp chia seeds
salt and pepper, optional

1. Put the red cabbage, carrot and cauliflower in a salad bowl. Add the apple, dried cranberries and shoots and toss well.

2. To make the dressing, put the walnuts in a large frying pan and toast for 2–3 minutes, or until just beginning to brown.

3. Put the orange juice, oil and chia seeds in a small bowl, season with salt and pepper, if using, then stir in the hot walnuts. Pour the dressing over the salad and toss gently. Serve immediately or cover and chill in the refrigerator until needed.

PER SERVING: 315 Kcals / 23.6g fat / 2.8g sat fat / 25.7g carbs / 15.3g sugar / 6.4g fibre / 4.8g protein / 0.1g salt

Basil & Lemon Cauliflower Rice

Raw cauliflower is pulsed in a food processor to resemble rice grains, then pan-fried with celery and garlic and combined with basil, lemon, watercress and hazelnuts to make this intriguing and nutritious side dish.

Serves 4

Prep: 20–25 minutes, plus cooling
Cook: 15–20 minutes

70 g/2½ oz skin-on hazelnuts, roughly chopped
500 g/1 lb 2 oz head of cauliflower
1 tbsp olive oil
2 celery sticks, roughly chopped
3 garlic cloves, roughly chopped
30 g/1 oz fresh basil, roughly chopped
zest and juice of 1 lemon
70 g/2½ oz watercress, chopped
salt and pepper, optional

1. Add the chopped hazelnuts to a large, dry frying pan. Toast over a medium heat until golden. Remove the hazelnuts from the pan and set aside.

2. Remove the core from the cauliflower and divide up the florets. Place in a food processor and pulse until the cauliflower resembles rice grains. Place in a bowl and set aside.

3. Place the olive oil in a frying pan over a medium heat and fry the celery and garlic for about 5–6 minutes, or until soft.

4. Add the cauliflower rice to the frying pan and stir to combine. Cook, stirring occasionally, for 8–10 minutes. Remove from the heat and allow the mixture to cool for a few minutes before adding the basil, lemon zest, lemon juice, toasted hazelnuts and watercress. Season with salt and pepper, if using, and serve immediately.

PER SERVING: *182 Kcals / 14.4g fat / 1.3g sat fat / 11.4g carbs / 3.7g sugar / 4.7g fibre / 5.7g protein / 0.1g salt*

Orzo with Mint & Fresh Tomatoes

Serves 4
Prep: 20 minutes
Cook: 20 minutes

350 g/12 oz orzo
125 g/4½ oz crème fraîche
150 g/5½ oz baby spinach
25 g/1 oz fresh mint, roughly chopped
300 g/10½ oz cherry
   tomatoes, roughly chopped
salt and pepper, optional
1 tbsp roughly chopped
   fresh mint, to garnish

Orzo pasta, which resembles fat grains of rice, pairs up with baby spinach and cherry tomatoes in this top-tasting salad that is finished with chopped mint leaves. A palate-pleasing and fresh-tasting meat-free side.

1. Bring a large saucepan of water to the boil and drop the orzo into the water. Stir vigorously to prevent the little grains sticking and then stir occasionally during cooking. Simmer for 8 minutes, or until the orzo is tender but still firm to the bite. Scoop out 100 ml/3 ½ fl oz of the cooking water and set aside.

2. Drain the orzo and return to the saucepan with the reserved cooking water. Place the pan over a very gentle heat and add the crème fraîche and spinach. Stir until the spinach has wilted and the crème fraîche has coated the grains. Remove from the heat.

3. Stir in the mint and cherry tomatoes. Season with salt and pepper, if using.

4. Garnish with mint and serve immediately.

PER SERVING: 443 Kcals / 11.4g fat / 7.1g sat fat / 70.9g carbs / 5.1g sugar / 5g fibre / 14g protein / 0.1g salt

Sprouting Broccoli with Pine Nuts

Serves 4
Prep: 25 minutes
Cook: 20–25 minutes

700 g/1 lb 9 oz purple
  sprouting broccoli
3 tbsp extra virgin olive oil
3 shallots, thinly sliced
2 large garlic cloves, thinly sliced
pinch of red chilli flakes
3 tbsp pine nuts, toasted
55 g/2 oz butter
2 tbsp capers, drained
4 tbsp snipped fresh chives
25 g/1 oz Parmesan cheese,
  shaved into wafers
salt and pepper, optional

A well-renowned superfood, purple sprouting broccoli forms the basis of this nutrient-busting, gluten-free side dish. High in healthy unsaturated fats, the toasted pine nuts add plenty of extra flavour and crunch too.

1. Cut off the broccoli florets and slice lengthways if thick. Slice the leaves and stems into 2-cm/¾-inch pieces. Steam for 2 minutes over a saucepan of boiling water, until barely soft. Remove from the heat. Reserve the cooking water.

2. Heat the oil in a large frying pan over a medium–low heat. Add the shallots and fry for 5 minutes.

3. Add the garlic and fry for 2–3 minutes, or until just starting to colour.

4. Increase the heat to medium and add the broccoli to the pan. Add the chilli flakes and season with salt and pepper, if using. Add 3–4 tablespoons of the broccoli cooking water. Cook and keep stirring for 4–6 minutes, or until the broccoli is just tender and the colour is still bright green.

5. Stir in the pine nuts and check the seasoning. Tip into a serving dish and keep warm.

6. Heat a heavy-based frying pan. When it is very hot, add the butter and sizzle until golden.

7. Remove from the heat and stir in the capers and half of the chives.

8. Pour the sauce over the broccoli. Sprinkle with the cheese shavings and the remaining chives.

PER SERVING: 331 Kcals / 28g fat / 9.9g sat fat / 16.1g carbs / 3.8g sugar / 5.3g fibre / 8.8g protein / 1g salt

Brown Rice with Pistachio Nuts, Parsley & Dried Cherries

Serves 4
Prep: 20 minutes, plus cooling
Cook: 30–35 minutes

400 g/14 oz brown rice
1 litre/1¾ pints vegetable stock
100 g/3½ oz dried cherries
1 small red onion, finely chopped
2 garlic cloves, crushed
4 tbsp roughly chopped fresh parsley
2 tbsp olive oil
100 g/3½ oz pistachio nuts,
   chopped
salt and pepper, optional
2 tbsp roughly chopped
   fresh parsley, to garnish

Full-of-fibre cooked brown rice is tossed with dried cherries and red onion, then finished with fresh parsley and chopped pistachios to create this energy-giving side that is suitable for vegetarians and vegans alike.

1. Place the rice into a large saucepan and cover well with the vegetable stock. Bring to a simmer and cook for 25 minutes, or until the rice is tender and nearly all of the stock has disappeared. Continue to simmer for a further few minutes if some stock remains.

2. Transfer the cooked rice to a large bowl and stir in the dried cherries, red onion and garlic. Season with salt and pepper, if using.

3. Allow the rice mixture to cool for a few minutes before adding the chopped parsley, olive oil and half of the pistachio nuts. Stir thoroughly until well combined.

4. Pile the warm rice mixture onto a serving dish and garnish with the remaining chopped pistachio nuts and the chopped parsley. Serve immediately.

PER SERVING: 684 Kcals / 22.9g fat / 3.9g sat fat / 108.1g carbs / 17.6g sugar / 7.7g fibre / 14.8g protein / 2.4g salt

Steamed Greens with Lemon & Coriander

Serves 4
Prep: 15 minutes
Cook: 6 minutes

*1 head of pointed spring cabbage,
  weighing about 450 g/1 lb,
  tough outer leaves discarded
200 g/7 oz baby spinach
large knob of unsalted butter
finely grated zest of ½ lemon
4 tbsp chopped fresh coriander
salt and pepper, optional*

This nutritious mix of lightly steamed greens tossed with butter, lemon zest and coriander is quick and easy to make.

1. Cut the cabbage in quarters lengthways and cut out the tough stalk. Slice the quarters crossways into 2-cm/¾-inch ribbons. Steam for 3 minutes, or until starting to soften.

2. Arrange the spinach on top of the cabbage, and steam for a further 3 minutes. Drain in a colander to remove any excess liquid.

3. Tip the cabbage and spinach into a warmed serving dish. Stir in the butter, lemon zest and coriander, mixing well.

4. Season with salt and pepper, if using, and serve immediately.

PER SERVING: *63 Kcals / 3.4g fat / 2g sat fat / 7.4g carbs / 4.2g sugar / 3.5g fibre / 2.7g protein / 0.1g salt*

Dressings, Sauces & Dips

Ginger, Garlic & Soy Dressing

Widely regarded for its anti-inflammatory properties, fresh ginger adds a lovely aromatic, spicy flavour to this Chinese-style dressing. For those who follow a gluten-free diet, be sure to use tamari or a gluten-free soy sauce.

Makes 150 ml / 5 fl oz
Prep: 10 minutes, plus chilling
Cook: No cooking

6-cm/2¼-inch piece of ginger, grated, juices reserved
2 garlic cloves, crushed
2 tbsp rice vinegar
2 tbsp dark soy sauce
1 tsp caster sugar
3 tbsp olive oil
2 tbsp water

1. Place the ginger in a screwtop jar with any juices. Add the garlic, rice vinegar, soy sauce, caster sugar, olive oil and water. Shake well until thoroughly combined.

2. Chill and store in the refrigerator until ready to use. This dressing improves with age so prepare the day before it is needed, if possible. This dressing goes well with a Chinese noodle salad or chopped Chinese leaves.

PER 150 ML/5 FL OZ: *400 Kcals / 40.5g fat / 5.6g sat fat / 8.6g carbs / 4.8g sugar / 0.4g fibre / 2.4g protein / 4.5g salt*

Tahini & Lemon Dressing

Tahini or sesame seed paste is full of essential nutrients, including healthy unsaturated fats and fibre. Combined with freshly squeezed lemon juice and flavoured with paprika and garlic, it forms a flavourful salad dressing.

Makes 300 ml/10 fl oz

Prep: 10 minutes
Cook: No cooking

100 g/3½ oz tahini
juice of 2 lemons (approximately 150 ml/5 fl oz)
4 tbsp water
¼ tsp paprika
1 garlic clove, crushed
pinch of salt

1. Put all of the ingredients in a food processor or blender and process until smooth. Add more paprika to taste, if desired.

2. If making by hand, thoroughly whisk together the tahini, lemon juice, water, paprika, garlic and salt in a bowl. You're aiming for a creamy, smooth texture. If it's too thick, add more water.

3. Serve immediately or place in a covered container in the refrigerator. This will keep in the refrigerator for up to 3 days. This dressing goes well with Greek salad.

PER 300 ML/10 FL OZ: 634 Kcals / 54.3g fat / 7.6g sat fat / 32.8g carbs / 4.4g sugar / 10g fibre / 17.8g protein / 1.8g salt

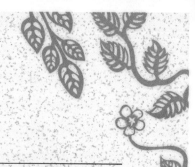

Avocado, Lemon & Paprika Dressing

Makes 300 ml / 10 fl oz

Prep: 15 minutes

Cook: No cooking

1 ripe avocado, roughly chopped
juice of a large lemon
1 small garlic clove
½ tsp paprika
75–100 ml/2½–3½ fl oz cold water

1. Put the avocado, lemon juice, garlic and paprika into a blender or food processor. Blitz until the mixture is well blended.

2. Slowly add the water until you reach the desired consistency. Pour the dressing into a jug and use as required.

3. This dressing can be made up to 3–4 hours in advance. Serve immediately or place in a covered container in the refrigerator for up to 1 day. This dressing goes well with salad or as a dip for chopped vegetables.

This flavour combination works really well together and could be a lovely dip to serve with root vegetable chips. Simply remove the cold water from the recipe.

PER 300 ML/10 FL OZ: *342 Kcals / 29.8g fat / 4.3g sat fat / 22.5g carbs / 3g sugar / 14.1g fibre / 4.5g protein / trace salt*

Garlic & Chilli Dipping Oil

Makes about 225 ml / 8 fl oz

Prep: 15 minutes, plus cooling

Cook: 1½–2 hours

5 garlic cloves, halved lengthways

2 tbsp deseeded and chopped jalapeño chilli

1 tsp dried oregano

225 ml / 8 fl oz rapeseed oil

1. Preheat the oven to 150°C/300°F/Gas Mark 2. Combine the garlic, chilli and oregano with the oil in an ovenproof glass measuring jug.

2. Place on a glass pie plate in the centre of the oven and heat for 1½–2 hours. The temperature of the oil should reach 120°C/250°F.

3. Using thick oven gloves, carefully remove the jug from the oven, allow to cool, then strain through muslin into a clean jar.

4. Store in an airtight container in the refrigerator for up to 1 month. You can also leave the garlic and chilli pieces in the oil and strain before using.

Be very careful during the heating of the oil stage in this recipe.

Lime & Miso Dressing

Makes 150 ml / 5 fl oz
Prep: 10 minutes, plus chilling
Cook: No cooking

1 tbsp fish sauce
1 tbsp rice vinegar
1 tbsp miso paste
grated zest and juice of 2 limes
2 tbsp sesame oil
2 tsp white sesame seeds
salt and pepper, optional

1. Place the fish sauce, rice vinegar, miso paste, lime juice and sesame oil in a screwtop jar. Add the lime zest and season with salt and pepper, if using.

2. Seal the jar and shake to mix thoroughly. Stir in the sesame seeds.

3. Chill in the refrigerator until ready to use. Drizzle over salads to serve.

This dressing could also be used as a lovely dipping sauce for dim sum or sushi.

PER 150 ML/5 FL OZ: 356 Kcals / 31.5g fat / 4.5g sat fat / 15.9g carbs / 3.7g sugar / 2.6g fibre / 5g protein / 5.8g salt

136

Wasabi & Soy Dressing

Makes 90 ml / 3 fl oz
Prep: 10 minutes
Cook: No cooking

3 tbsp groundnut oil

juice of ½ lime

1 tsp wasabi paste

1 tbsp soy sauce

1 tsp sesame oil

½ tsp dark brown sugar

1 tbsp rice wine vinegar

1. Place all of the ingredients into a small bowl. Whisk the mixture together with a fork until all of the sugar has dissolved.

2. Serve the dressing immediately to drizzle over salads. This dressing goes particularly well with plain salads that need pepping up with a bit of heat.

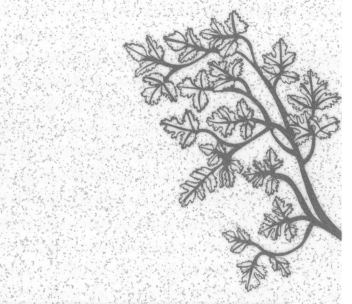

For extra zing, add the finely grated zest of a lemon to the dressing.

Caper & Oregano Vinaigrette

Extra virgin olive oil, which is naturally high in healthy monounsaturated fat and low in saturated fat, is the top oil to pick for this herb-packed vinaigrette. Capers add extra distinctive flavour and appeal too.

Makes 125 ml / 4 fl oz
Prep: 15 minutes
Cook: No cooking

juice of 2 lemons
1 tbsp finely chopped capers
2 tbsp finely chopped fresh oregano
2 garlic cloves, crushed
4 tbsp extra virgin olive oil
pinch of soft brown sugar
salt and pepper, optional

1. Simply squeeze the lemon juice into a small jug and stir in the capers, oregano, garlic, olive oil and brown sugar. Whisk well and season with salt and pepper, if using.

2. Serve immediately or place in a covered container and keep in the refrigerator for up to 1 month. This goes well with any salad or drizzled over mozzarella cheese.

PER 125 ML/4 FL OZ: 519 Kcals / 54.4g fat / 7.5g sat fat / 11.6g carbs / 3.8g sugar / 1.5g fibre / 1.1g protein / 0.6g salt

Healthy Caesar Dressing

Low-fat natural yogurt and reduced-fat mayo combine to provide the perfect basis for this lighter, healthy alternative to Caesar dressing that is filled with flavour from the anchovies, garlic, lemon and parsley.

Makes 125 ml / 4 fl oz

Prep: 15 minutes

Cook: No cooking

100 g/3½ oz low-fat Greek-style natural yogurt

3 anchovy fillets, roughly chopped

2 garlic cloves, crushed

grated zest and juice from ½ lemon

25 g/1 oz fresh flat-leaf parsley, roughly chopped

1 tbsp low-fat mayonnaise

1. Place all of the ingredients, except the mayonnaise, in a small bowl and pulse with a hand-held blender until the parsley and anchovies have disintegrated. As the parsley breaks down, the dressing will take on a beautiful green colour and become easier to blend.

2. Stir in the mayonnaise. Serve immediately as an alternative to Caesar dressing. This will also keep for 3–4 days in a covered container in the refrigerator.

PER 125 ML/4 FL OZ: *147 Kcals / 5.3g fat / 0.7g sat fat / 10.6g carbs / 5g sugar / 1.2g fibre / 15g protein / 1.5g salt*

Slow-cooked Tomato Pasta Sauce

Makes 750 ml / 1¼ pints

Prep: 20 minutes, plus cooling
Cook: 1 hour 40 minutes

50 ml/2 fl oz olive oil
1 onion, chopped
5 garlic cloves, finely sliced
2 tbsp roughly chopped fresh flat-leaf parsley
2 tbsp roughly chopped fresh basil
1.5 kg/3 lb 5 oz tomatoes, cored and roughly chopped
1 tsp brown sugar
1 tbsp red wine vinegar
salt and pepper, optional

1. Heat the olive oil in a heavy-based saucepan over a medium heat. Add the onion and fry gently until it softens and turns almost golden.

2. Add the garlic and herbs and fry for 30 seconds before carefully pouring in the chopped tomatoes, including the seeds and skin. Stir in the sugar and vinegar. Season with salt and pepper, if using, then reduce the heat to medium–low and simmer the sauce, uncovered, for 1½ hours, or until the tomatoes have broken down and the sauce has thickened. Stir occasionally to prevent anything catching on the bottom of the pan. At the end, season again with salt and pepper, if using.

3. Allow to cool slightly and serve mixed into pasta or spaghetti, or as required. If you like your sauce to be a little smoother, simply blend using a food processor or hand-held blender.

Once made, this sauce can be divided into containers and frozen for up to 3 months.

PER 750 ML/1¼ PINTS: 805 Kcals / 53.3g fat / 7.3g sat fat / 79.2g carbs / 49.3g sugar / 20.6g fibre / 15.7g protein / 0.2g salt

142

Avocado & Cashew Nut Pasta Sauce

Makes 400 ml / 14 fl oz
Prep: 20 minutes
Cook: 3–4 minutes

100 g / 3½ oz cashew nuts
2 garlic cloves, chopped
30 g / 1 oz fresh mint, leaves picked
2 perfectly ripe avocados, roughly chopped
50 g / 1¾ oz Parmesan cheese, finely grated
2 tbsp olive oil
juice of 1 lime
1–2 tbsp water

1. Toast the cashews in a dry frying pan over a high heat for 3–4 minutes, moving the pan regularly to prevent the nuts from burning.

2. Place the cashew nuts and garlic cloves in a food processor and pulse until the nuts are finely chopped. Add the mint leaves, avocados and Parmesan cheese. Blend and, with the motor running, pour in the olive oil and lime juice. Add just enough water to reach a thick sauce consistency.

3. Use immediately or keep in the refrigerator in a covered container. The sauce will keep for up to 2 days. Serve mixed into pasta.

This recipe relies on perfectly ripe avocados
– to ripen a hard avocado, place it in a paper bag
with a banana or an apple overnight.

PER 400 ML/14 FL OZ: 1666 Kcals / 142.9g fat / 28.4g sat fat / 74.1g carbs / 9.8g sugar / 32.6g fibre / 45.7g protein / 2g salt

Beetroot &
Hazelnut Pesto

Serves 8
Prep: 20–25 minutes, plus cooling
Cook: 1 hour

250 g/9 oz raw beetroot
100 ml/3½ fl oz extra virgin olive oil
115 g/4 oz roasted hazelnuts
2 garlic cloves, peeled
115 g/4 oz fresh Parmesan cheese, freshly grated
salt and pepper, optional

1. Preheat the oven to 180°C/ 350°F/Gas Mark 4.

2. Sprinkle the beetroot with a little salt and pepper, if using, then drizzle with a small amount of the olive oil. Wrap the beetroot in foil and place in the oven. Cook for 1 hour. To test to see if the beetroot is cooked, poke with a small knife; the blade should go in with ease.

3. Remove the cooked beetroot from the oven and leave to cool. Once cool, peel away the skin and discard.

4. Place the hazelnuts and garlic in a food processor and process for 30 seconds.

5. Add the beetroot and salt and pepper, if using, and process again adding the remaining olive oil a little at a time, through the feeder tube, until combined.

6. Transfer the pesto to a medium bowl and mix in the Parmesan cheese.

7. This pesto can be served with crudités or mixed into pasta or spaghetti.

This is a great alternative to basil pesto, adding nutrients with the beetroot and nuts.

PER SERVING: *274 Kcals / 25.2g fat / 4.7g sat fat / 6.2g carbs / 2.9g sugar / 2.2g fibre / 7.8g protein / 0.6g salt*

Beetroot & Cucumber Tzatziki on Salad Leaves

Serves 4
Prep: 20 minutes
Cook: No cooking

115 g/4 oz cooked beetroot in natural juices
   (drained weight), drained and diced
150 g/5½ oz cucumber, diced
40 g/1½ oz radishes, diced
1 spring onion, finely chopped
12 Little Gem lettuce leaves

Dressing
150 g/5½ oz low-fat Greek-style natural yogurt
¼ tsp ground cumin
½ tsp runny honey
2 tbsp finely chopped fresh mint
salt and pepper, optional

1. To make the dressing, put the yogurt, cumin and honey in a bowl. Stir in the mint and season with salt and pepper, if using.

2. Add the beetroot, cucumber, radishes and spring onion, then toss gently together.

3. Arrange the lettuce leaves on a plate. Spoon a little of the tzatziki into each leaf. Serve immediately.

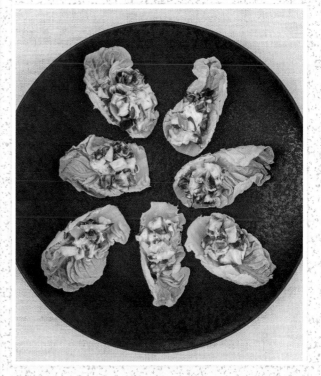

These are perfect for serving as canapés or as a sharing snack with friends.

PER SERVING: 51 Kcals / 0.2g fat / 0g sat fat / 8.2g carbs / 5.7g sugar / 1.8g fibre / 5.1g protein / 0.1g salt

Guacamole Dip

Crammed with creamy avocado flesh, this popular dip is also jam-packed with nutrients including heart-friendly monounsaturated fat and vitamin C, plus it can be enjoyed by allergy sufferers and vegans too.

Serves 4

Prep: 15 minutes
Cook: No cooking

2 large avocados, sliced
juice of 2 limes
2 large garlic cloves, crushed
1 tsp mild chilli powder
salt and pepper, optional
1 tsp mild chilli powder, to garnish

1. Put the avocado slices, lime juice, garlic and chilli powder in a food processor and process until smooth. Season with salt and pepper, if using.

2. Transfer to a serving bowl, garnish with chilli powder and serve immediately.

Baba Ghanoush

Serves 6
Prep: 20 minutes, plus cooling
Cook: 1 hour

2 large aubergines
1 garlic clove, chopped
2 tsp ground cumin
4 tbsp tahini
2 tbsp lemon juice
4 tbsp natural yogurt
2 tbsp chopped fresh coriander
1 tbsp chopped fresh coriander, to garnish

1. Preheat the oven to 220°C/425°F/Gas Mark 7.
Prick the aubergine skins and place them on a baking
sheet. Bake in the preheated oven for 1 hour, or until very
soft. Remove from the oven and set aside to cool.

2. Peel off and discard the aubergine skins. Coarsely
chop the flesh and place it in a food processor. Add the
garlic, cumin, tahini, lemon juice, yogurt and coriander
and process until smooth and combined, scraping down
the sides as necessary.

3. Transfer to a serving dish, garnish with a little
coriander and serve. If you are preparing this ahead of
serving, cover the dish tightly with clingfilm and store in
the refrigerator until 30 minutes before serving.

*This dip is a classic Middle Eastern mezze dish and tastes great
when served with pitta bread.*

PER SERVING: *107 Kcals / 6.1g fat / 1g sat fat / 12.2g carbs / 4.3g sugar / 6.3g fibre / 3.8g protein / trace salt*

Basil & Raw Garlic Hummus

Serves 4

Prep: 15–20 minutes

Cook: No cooking

400 g/14 oz canned chickpeas, drained and rinsed

3 tbsp tahini

30 g/1 oz fresh basil, roughly chopped

pinch of paprika

2 garlic cloves

finely grated zest and juice of 1 lemon

4–5 tbsp cold water

salt and pepper, optional

30 g/1 oz fresh basil sprigs, to garnish

1. Place the chickpeas, tahini, basil, paprika, garlic cloves and lemon zest and juice in a food processor. Process to a coarse mixture.

2. With the food processor still running, slowly add the cold water until a smooth, thick paste is formed, adding a little more if needed. Season with salt and pepper, if using.

3. Garnish with basil and serve immediately or place in a covered container and keep in the refrigerator. This will keep in the refrigerator for up to 3 days.

Hummus can have so many different variations so once you have the staple chickpea, tahini and garlic version sorted, try adding different flavours; harissa or olives also work well.

PER SERVING: 152 Kcals / 7.3g fat / 1g sat fat / 15g carbs / 3.4g sugar / 5.3g fibre / 6.4g protein / trace salt

Broad Bean & Mint Hummus with Crudités

Serves 4

Prep: 30–35 minutes

Cook: 15 minutes

350 g/12 oz podded broad beans

2 tbsp virgin olive oil

1 tsp cumin seeds, crushed

3 spring onions, thinly sliced

2 garlic cloves, finely chopped

25 g/1 oz fresh mint,
   torn into pieces

25 g/1 oz fresh flat-leaf
   parsley, finely chopped

juice of 1 lemon

60 g/2¼ oz Greek-style
   natural yogurt

salt and pepper, optional

To serve

1 red and 1 yellow pepper,
   deseeded and cut into strips

4 celery sticks, cut into strips

½ cucumber, halved, deseeded
   and cut into strips

4 pitta breads, cut into strips, optional

Broad beans are an excellent vegetable source of protein and fibre, so when combined with fresh garden herbs and garlic, they make a great-tasting healthy hummus that's just right served with colourful raw vegetable crudités.

1. Half-fill the base of a steamer with water. Bring the steamer to the boil, then put the broad beans in the steamer top. Cover with a lid and steam for 10 minutes, or until tender.

2. Meanwhile, heat the oil in a frying pan over a medium heat. Add the cumin, spring onions and garlic, and cook for 2 minutes, or until the onion is softened.

3. Put the beans in a food processor or blender, add the onion mixture, herbs, lemon juice and yogurt and season with salt and pepper, if using. Process to a coarse purée, then spoon into a dish set on a large plate.

4. Arrange the vegetable strips around the hummus and serve with the pittas, if using.

PER SERVING: 202 Kcals / 8.6g fat / 1.5g sat fat / 17.3g carbs / 4.6g sugar / 8.1g fibre / 9.8g protein / 0.1g salt

A Feast
of Vegetables

Mushrooms & Squash on Buckwheat

Serves 4
Prep: 25 minutes
Cook: 40–45 minutes

1 kg/2 lb 4 oz squash, such as
  Crown Prince or Kabocha
1 tbsp thick balsamic vinegar
125 ml/4 fl oz olive oil
large knob of butter
225 g/8 oz roasted
  buckwheat, rinsed
1 egg, lightly beaten
450 ml/15 fl oz vegetable stock
1 onion, halved and sliced
250 g/9 oz small chestnut
  mushrooms, quartered
2 tbsp lemon juice
6 tbsp chopped fresh
  flat-leaf parsley
25 g/1 oz walnut halves,
  roughly chopped
salt and pepper, optional

Buckwheat is naturally gluten-free and provides a balanced base for this very tempting vegetable dish. Roasted squash adds important antioxidants, while walnuts add a bit of crunch and health-benefiting omega-3 fatty acids.

1. Preheat the oven to 200°C/400°F/ Gas Mark 6. Cut the squash into eight wedges, peel and deseed.

2. Put the squash into a roasting tin and toss with the vinegar and 6 tablespoons of the oil. Season with salt and pepper, if using, and dot with the butter. Roast in the preheated oven for 25–30 minutes, until slightly caramelized.

3. Meanwhile, put the buckwheat into a large frying pan. Add the egg, stirring to coat the grains. Stir over a medium heat for 3 minutes, or until the egg moisture has evaporated. Add the stock and simmer gently for 9–10 minutes, or until the grains are tender but not disintegrating. Remove the pan from the heat and set the buckwheat aside.

4. Heat the remaining oil in the frying pan. Add the onion and fry over a medium heat for 10 minutes. Season with salt and pepper, if using. Add the mushrooms and fry for 5 minutes. Stir in the buckwheat, lemon juice and most of the parsley.

5. Transfer the buckwheat mixture to four plates and arrange the squash on top. Scatter over the walnuts and the remaining parsley. Serve immediately.

PER SERVING: 662 Kcals / 42.1g fat / 7.8g sat fat / 67.6g carbs / 7.9g sugar / 10.3g fibre / 13.2g protein / 1.2g salt

Courgette Spaghetti

Courgettes create simple strips of spaghetti, which are then lightly cooked and tossed with pesto, roasted tomatoes, garlic and feta cheese in this inspiring, nourishing dish. Toasted sunflower seeds add some vital vitamin E too.

Serves 2

Prep: 30 minutes
Cook: 25–27 minutes

150 g/5½ oz cherry tomatoes
4 garlic cloves, sliced
1 tbsp olive oil
50 g/1¾ oz sunflower seeds
2 large courgettes
2 tbsp fresh pesto
70 g/2½ oz feta cheese, crumbled
salt and pepper, optional
25 g/1 oz fresh basil, roughly chopped, to garnish

1. Preheat the oven to 200°C/400°F/Gas Mark 6. Cut half of the cherry tomatoes in half horizontally and leave the rest whole. Place all the tomatoes and sliced garlic into a small roasting tin and drizzle over the olive oil. Shake well to coat and place in the preheated oven for 20 minutes.

2. Meanwhile, place a dry frying pan over a medium heat. Add the sunflower seeds and fry for 3–4 minutes, or until the seeds are just toasted. Set aside.

3. Now make your courgette spaghetti. Lay a box grater on its side and grate the length of the courgette into long strands. Try not to be firm – a loose grip makes this easier.

4. Bring a saucepan of water to the boil and add the courgette strips. Cook for 1–2 minutes before draining thoroughly in a colander, gently squeezing any excess water away with the back of a spoon. Return the spaghetti to the pan and stir through the pesto. Season with salt and pepper, if using.

5. Stir two thirds of the roasted tomato mixture, half of the sunflower seeds and half of the crumbled feta into the spaghetti and divide the mixture between two plates. Top with the remaining tomatoes, sunflower seeds, and feta. Garnish with the basil and a sprinkling of black pepper, if using. Serve immediately.

PER SERVING: 464 Kcals / 37.8g fat / 9.7g sat fat / 19.9g carbs / 10.9g sugar / 6g fibre / 16.7g protein / 1.5g salt

Raw Shoots & Seeds Super Salad

Serves 6
Prep: 20 minutes
Cook: No cooking

225 g/8 oz mixed sprouted seeds and
   beans (alfalfa, mung beans,
   soy beans, aduki beans,
   chickpeas and radish seeds)
25 g/1 oz pumpkin seeds
25 g/1 oz sunflower seeds
25 g/1 oz sesame seeds
1 dessert apple, cored and
   roughly chopped
70 g/2½ oz dried apricots,
   roughly chopped
finely grated zest and juice of 1 lemon
50 g/1¾ oz walnuts, roughly chopped
2 tbsp walnut oil

Help your body to rebalance with this nutritious and delicious meat-free, gluten-free salad. Bursting with healthy sprouted and dried seeds, walnuts and fruit, this top-pick salad is tossed together in a light lemony dressing.

1. Put the sprouted seeds, pumpkin seeds, sunflower seeds and sesame seeds in a large bowl. Stir in the apple, dried apricots, lemon zest and walnuts.

2. To make the dressing, put the lemon juice and oil in a small bowl and mix together with a fork.

3. Stir the dressing into the salad, then serve immediately.

PER SERVING: *221 Kcals / 16.4g fat / 1.8g sat fat / 17.1g carbs / 11g sugar / 3.9g fibre / 5.8g protein / trace salt*

Black Bean & Quinoa Burritos

Makes 8

Prep: 25–30 minutes, plus standing
Cook: 30–35 minutes

60 g/2¼ oz red quinoa, rinsed

150 ml/5 fl oz water

2 tbsp vegetable oil

1 red onion, diced

1 fresh green chilli,
    deseeded and diced

1 small red pepper,
    deseeded and diced

400 g/14 oz canned black
    beans, drained and rinsed

juice of 1 lime

4 tbsp chopped fresh coriander

2 tomatoes

8 corn tortillas, warmed

125 g/4½ oz Cheddar
    cheese, coarsely grated

85 g/3 oz shredded cos lettuce

salt and pepper, optional

Quinoa and black beans boost the protein and fibre in these brilliant burritos, finished with salsa and calcium-rich Cheddar.

1. Put the quinoa into a saucepan with the water. Bring to the boil, then cover and simmer over a very low heat for 15 minutes. Remove from the heat, but leave the pan covered for a further 5 minutes to allow the grains to swell. Fluff up with a fork and set aside.

2. Heat the oil in a large frying pan. Fry half of the onion, half of the chilli and all of the red pepper until soft. Add the beans, cooked quinoa and half of the lime juice and coriander. Cook, stirring, for a few minutes, then season with salt and pepper, if using.

3. Halve the tomatoes and scoop out the seeds. Add the seeds to the bean mixture. Dice the tomato flesh and place in a bowl with the remaining coriander, onion, chilli, lime juice and salt, if using. Stir.

4. Place 5 tablespoons of the bean mixture on top of each tortilla. Sprinkle with the tomato salsa, the cheese and lettuce. Fold the end and sides over the filling, roll up and serve immediately.

PER BURRITO: *291 Kcals / 11.4g fat / 4.7g sat fat / 34.3g carbs / 4.5g sugar / 5.8g fibre / 11.4g protein / 0.7g salt*

Aubergines Stuffed with Bulgar Wheat

A good source of vitamins, minerals and fibre, purple-skinned aubergines are great for stuffing and work well with spices in this wholesome dish. Fibre-rich bulgar wheat provides a good basis for the herby-vegetable stuffing too.

Serves 4

Prep: 35 minutes, plus resting
Cook: 50 minutes

1 tsp ground cumin
1 tsp ground coriander
1 tsp paprika
1 tsp chilli flakes
2 tbsp olive oil
2 aubergines, cut in half lengthways
1 red onion, roughly chopped
2 garlic cloves, chopped
150 g/5½ oz fine bulgar wheat
200 ml/7 fl oz vegetable stock
3 tbsp roughly chopped fresh coriander
3 tbsp roughly chopped fresh mint
125 g/4½ oz feta cheese, crumbled
30 g/1 oz flaked almonds, toasted
1½ tbsp lemon juice

2 tsp pomegranate molasses
salt and pepper, optional
1 tbsp chopped fresh mint, to garnish
1 tsp pomegranate molasses, to garnish
125 g/4½ oz Greek-style natural yogurt, to garnish
4 tbsp pomegranate seeds, to garnish

1. Preheat the oven to 180°C/350°F/Gas Mark 4. Mix the cumin, ground coriander, paprika, chilli flakes and 1½ tablespoons of olive oil in a small bowl. Use a sharp knife to slice the aubergine flesh in a diagonal, criss-cross pattern, being careful not to pierce the skin. Drizzle the cumin mixture over the aubergines and allow it to sink into the criss-crosses. Place the aubergine halves on a baking sheet and roast in the preheated oven for 35 minutes.

PER SERVING: *451 Kcals / 20.7g fat / 7.3g sat fat / 55.2g carbs / 12.6g sugar / 18.6g fibre / 17.5g protein / 1.4g salt*

2. Meanwhile, heat the remaining half a tablespoon of olive oil in a large frying pan over a medium heat. Add the onion and garlic and fry for about 3–4 minutes, or until softened. Reduce the heat, add the bulgar wheat and stir well. Reduce the heat to low, pour over the vegetable stock and continue to stir until the liquid has been absorbed. Remove this mixture from the pan and transfer to a large bowl.

3. Remove the aubergines from the oven and leave to rest for 10 minutes, or until cool enough to handle. Leave the oven on. Using a dessertspoon, scoop out the centre of the aubergine, leaving a clear edge to support the filling.

4. Add the aubergine flesh to the bulgar mixture. Stir in the fresh coriander, mint, feta, almonds, lemon juice and pomegranate molasses. Stir well and season with salt and pepper, if using.

5. Divide the stuffing between the aubergines and return to the oven for 15 minutes. Serve immediately, garnished with the fresh mint, molasses, yogurt and pomegranate seeds.

Butternut Squash & Lentil Stew

Serves 4
Prep: 20 minutes
Cook: 35 minutes

1 tbsp olive oil

1 onion, diced

3 garlic cloves, finely chopped

2 tbsp tomato purée

2 tsp ground cumin

1 tsp ground cinnamon

1 tsp salt

¼ tsp cayenne pepper

450 g/1 lb butternut squash, peeled, deseeded and cut into bite-sized pieces

100 g/3½ oz brown lentils

450 ml/16 fl oz vegetable stock

1 tbsp lemon juice

4 tbsp natural yogurt, to garnish

2 tbsp finely chopped fresh coriander, to garnish

2 tbsp flaked almonds, to garnish

Naturally low in fat, lentils are packed with fibre and protein and are a good source of iron and other minerals. Teamed up with antioxidant-rich butternut squash, this super vegetarian stew packs a powerful nutrient punch.

1. Heat the oil in a large saucepan over a medium–high heat. Add the onion and garlic and cook, stirring occasionally, for about 5 minutes, or until soft.

2. Add the tomato purée, cumin, cinnamon, salt and cayenne and give it a quick stir. Add the squash, lentils and stock to the pan and bring to the boil.

3. Reduce the heat to low and simmer, uncovered and stirring occasionally, for about 25 minutes, or until the squash and lentils are tender.

4. Just before serving, stir in the lemon juice. Serve hot, garnished with a dollop of the yogurt and a sprinkling of coriander and flaked almonds.

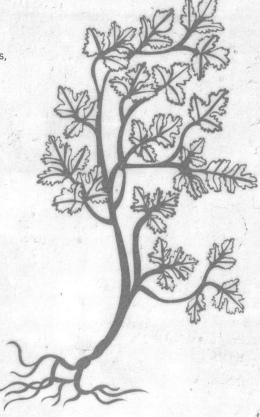

PER SERVING: *238 Kcals / 7.6g fat / 1.5g sat fat / 36.5g carbs / 6.4g sugar / 11.7g fibre / 9.7g protein / 2.6g salt*

Multi-grain & Sprouting Seeds Salad

Serves 4
Prep: 30–35 minutes, plus cooling
Cook: 30–35 minutes

700 ml/1¼ pints vegetable stock
40 g/1½ oz wild rice
115 g/4 oz bulgar wheat
115 g/4 oz quinoa
2 courgettes, diagonally sliced
4 spring onions, halved lengthways
4 tbsp olive oil
juice of ½ lemon
1 tsp cumin seeds, roughly crushed
25 g/1 oz fresh flat-leaf
   parsley, roughly chopped
50 g/1¾ oz mixed
   ready-to-eat sprouting seeds, such
   as alfalfa and radish sprouts
salt and pepper, optional

Dressing

finely grated zest and juice
   of ½ unwaxed lemon
finely grated zest and juice of 1 lime
1 tsp runny honey

Health-giving grains, plenty of griddled vegetables, plus vitamin-rich sprouting seeds are packed into this satisfying and sustaining salad. A light and zesty lemon and lime dressing brings it all together perfectly.

1. Bring the stock to the boil in a saucepan, add the rice and simmer for 5 minutes. Add the bulgar wheat and simmer for 5 minutes more. Add the quinoa and simmer for 10–12 minutes, or until all the grains are tender. Drain off and discard the stock and spoon the grains into a salad bowl.

2. To make the dressing, put the lemon and lime zest and juices, honey and 2 tablespoons of the olive oil in a jam jar. Season with salt and pepper, if using, screw on the lid and shake well. Drizzle over the grains, toss gently together, then leave to cool.

3. Meanwhile, mix the courgettes and onions with the remaining 2 tablespoons of olive oil, the lemon juice and cumin and season with salt and pepper, if using.

4. Preheat a ridged griddle pan over a high heat. Cook the courgettes and onion in the hot pan for 1–2 minutes on each side, or until browned. Transfer to a plate and leave to cool. Serve the grains on four plates and top with the griddled vegetables. Top with the parsley and sprouting seeds and serve.

PER SERVING: 416 Kcals / 17.4g fat / 2.9g sat fat / 58.1g carbs / 6.6g sugar / 10g fibre / 11.8g protein / 1.7g salt

Cashew & Chickpea Curry

Serves 4
Prep: 15 minutes
Cook: 40–45 minutes

150 g/5½ oz potatoes, chopped
   into bite-sized pieces
3 tbsp vegetable oil
1 onion, chopped
2 garlic cloves, chopped
3-cm/1¼-inch piece fresh ginger,
   finely chopped
1 tsp cumin seeds
1 tsp chilli powder
½ tsp ground turmeric
½ tsp ground cinnamon
400 g/14 oz canned chickpeas,
   drained and rinsed
150 g/5½ oz cashew nuts
350 ml/12 fl oz vegetable stock
100 g/3½ oz creamed coconut
1 tbsp chopped fresh
   coriander, to garnish
400 g/14 oz freshly
   cooked rice, to serve

Crammed with chickpeas and cashew nuts, this tasty curry is brimming with essential nutrients including fibre and protein.

1. Place the potatoes in a large saucepan of boiling water and cook for 10–15 minutes, until tender but still firm.

2. Heat the oil in a large saucepan over a medium heat. Fry the onion, garlic, ginger, cumin seeds, chilli powder, turmeric and cinnamon for 5 minutes, or until the onion is soft and translucent.

3. Stir in the boiled potatoes, chickpeas and cashews, and cook for a further 3 minutes. Stir in the stock and the creamed coconut and stir until the coconut melts into the dish. Reduce the heat to low and continue to cook for 15 minutes, or until thick and creamy.

4. Garnish with coriander and serve immediately with the freshly cooked rice on the side.

PER SERVING: 720 Kcals / 44.7g fat / 19.5g sat fat / 62.8g carbs / 8.8g sugar / 7.3g fibre / 16.5g protein / 0.9g salt

Whole Baked Cauliflower

Low-fat, cholesterol-free and loaded with vitamin C, cauliflower is baked whole and served with a tasty tomato, olive and caper sauce. Fibre and protein-packed butter beans add to the mix in this warming supper dish.

Serves 4

Prep: 20–25 minutes
Cook: 1 hour

1 tbsp olive oil
2 onions, finely sliced
4 garlic cloves, chopped
2 tbsp red wine vinegar
pinch of soft brown sugar
70 g/2½ oz black olives, pitted
2 tbsp capers
3 tbsp roughly chopped fresh basil
800 g/1 lb 12 oz canned chopped tomatoes
400 g/14 oz canned butter beans, drained and rinsed
150 ml/5 fl oz vegetable stock
1 large cauliflower, leaves trimmed
salt and pepper, optional
2 tbsp basil sprigs, to garnish

1. Heat the olive oil in a saucepan that is large enough to fit the whole cauliflower in.

2. Add the onions and garlic and fry, over a medium heat, until soft and translucent. Stir in the vinegar, brown sugar, black olives, capers and basil and heat through for a further 2–3 minutes. Pour in the tomatoes, butter beans and vegetable stock. Stir well and bring the saucepan to a simmer for 5–6 minutes, stirring occasionally.

3. Sit the cauliflower head upside down on a chopping board and, using a sharp knife, carefully cut the tough stem away. Place the cauliflower into the centre of the tomato sauce, pushing it down so half is covered by the sauce. Season with salt and pepper, if using.

4. Reduce the heat to low, cover and simmer for approximately 45 minutes, or until the cauliflower is tender. Carefully stir once or twice during cooking to prevent the sauce catching on the base of the pan. Serve immediately, garnished with basil.

PER SERVING: *242 Kcals / 7.3g fat / 1g sat fat / 34.6g carbs / 14.2g sugar / 9.6g fibre / 11.5g protein / 1.1g salt*

Brown Rice Risotto Primavera

Serves 4
Prep: 25 minutes
Cook: 45 minutes

1.2 litres/2 pints vegetable stock

1 tbsp olive oil

1 large leek, thinly sliced, white
and green slices kept separate

2 garlic cloves, finely chopped

250 g/9 oz short-grain brown rice

150 g/5½ oz baby carrots, tops
trimmed, halved lengthways

100 g/3½ oz asparagus spears,
woody stems removed

225 g/8 oz courgettes, cut into cubes

25 g/1 oz butter

70 g/2½ oz Parmesan
cheese, finely grated

60 g/2¼ oz mixed baby spinach,
watercress and rocket leaves

Loaded with fresh spring vegetables for vitality, this brown rice risotto provides a delicious and balanced meat-free meal.

1. Bring the stock to the boil in a saucepan.

2. Meanwhile, heat the oil in a large frying pan over a medium heat. Add the white leek slices and garlic and cook for 3–4 minutes, or until softened but not browned.

3. Stir the rice into the pan and cook for 1 minute. Pour in half of the hot stock, bring back to the boil, then cover and simmer for 15 minutes.

4. Add the carrots and half of the remaining stock and stir again. Cover and cook for 15 minutes.

5. Add the green leek slices, asparagus and courgettes to the rice, then add a little extra stock. Re-cover and cook for 5–6 minutes, or until the vegetables and rice are just tender.

6. Remove from the heat, stir in the butter and two-thirds of the cheese, and add a little more stock if needed. Top with the mixed leaves, cover with the lid, and warm through for 1–2 minutes, or until the leaves are just beginning to wilt.

7. Spoon the risotto into shallow bowls, sprinkle with the remaining cheese and serve immediately.

PER SERVING: *433 Kcals / 16.8g fat / 8.1g sat fat / 59.6g carbs / 5.4g sugar / 5g fibre / 13.6g protein / 3.7g salt*

Tagliatelle with Roasted Pumpkin

Home-made pesto is hard to beat and no more so than with this walnut-loaded version, rich in essential omega-3 fatty acids and heart-healthy monounsaturated fat, and tossed with wholewheat tagliatelle and roasted pumpkin.

Serves 4
Prep: 35–40 minutes
Cook: 30–35 minutes

1 kg/2 lb 4 oz pumpkin or butternut squash, deseeded, peeled and cut into 2-cm/¾-inch slices
2 tbsp virgin olive oil
500 g/1 lb 2 oz fresh wholewheat tagliatelle
salt and pepper, optional
1 tbsp thinly shaved Parmesan cheese, to serve

Walnut pesto
85 g/3 oz walnuts, broken into pieces
6 tbsp virgin olive oil
15 g/½ oz fresh basil
25 g/1 oz Parmesan cheese, thinly shaved
70 g/2½ oz rocket leaves

1. Preheat the oven to 200°C/400°F/Gas Mark 6. Arrange the pumpkin on a large baking sheet in a single layer. Drizzle with the oil and season with salt and pepper, if using. Roast for 20–25 minutes, or until just tender.

2. Meanwhile, to make the pesto, put the walnuts in a large frying pan and toast for 2–3 minutes, or until just beginning to brown. Transfer to a food processor or blender, pour in the oil and process until coarsely ground. Add the basil, cheese and half of the rocket leaves and process again until you have a coarse pesto.

3. Bring a large saucepan of water to the boil, add the tagliatelle and cook for 3–4 minutes, or according to the packet instructions, until al dente.

4. Drain the pasta and pour a little of the cooking water into a jug. Return the pasta to the pan. Cut the pumpkin into cubes and add this to the pasta. Drizzle over the pesto and gently toss together, adding a little of the reserved pasta water if needed to loosen the sauce. Top with the remaining rocket.

5. Spoon into bowls and serve immediately, with the Parmesan cheese on top.

PER SERVING: *912 Kcals / 44.9g fat / 6.7g sat fat / 113.9g carbs / 9.3g sugar / 13g fibre / 27.2g protein / 0.3g salt*

High-fibre Green Lentil & Egg Salad

Serves 4
Prep: 30 minutes, plus cooling
Cook: 40–45 minutes

850 ml/1½ pints vegetable stock
2 bay leaves
1 cinnamon stick, halved
225 g/8 oz leeks
225 g/8 oz green lentils,
    rinsed and drained
3 tbsp olive oil
2 garlic cloves, finely chopped
4 eggs
2 tbsp capers, drained and chopped
85 g/3 oz baby spinach
25 g/1 oz fresh flat-leaf parsley,
    roughly chopped

Dressing
2 tbsp red wine vinegar
1 tsp Dijon mustard
salt and pepper, optional

Packed with fibre, lentils add a healthy, low-fat source of protein to this tempting mixed vegetable and egg salad, finished with a drizzle of piquant mustard dressing and sprinkled with antioxidant-rich fresh parsley.

1. Put the stock, bay and cinnamon in a saucepan and bring just to the boil. Cut a 7.5-cm/3-inch piece from the white base of one of the leeks and add this and the lentils to the pan. Cover and simmer for 25 minutes, or until the lentils are tender and nearly all the stock has been absorbed. Top up with a little boiling water during cooking if needed. Drain the lentils, transfer to a salad bowl and discard the cooked leek, bay leaves and cinnamon stick.

2. Meanwhile, thinly slice the rest of the leeks. Heat 1 tablespoon of olive oil in a frying pan over a medium heat. Add the sliced leeks and the garlic and fry for 3–4 minutes, stirring, until just beginning to soften. Remove from the heat and leave to cool.

3. Put the eggs in a saucepan and pour in enough cold water to cover them by 1 cm/½ inch. Bring to the boil, then reduce the heat and boil for 8 minutes. Drain immediately, cool by quickly placing the eggs under cold running water, then peel and cut into quarters.

4. To make the dressing, put the vinegar, remaining 2 tablespoons of oil and the mustard in a jam jar. Season with salt and pepper, if using, screw on the lid and shake well.

5. Drizzle the dressing over the lentils and toss gently together. Top with the sliced leek mixture, capers and spinach. Arrange the hard-boiled eggs over the salad, sprinkle with the chopped parsley and serve immediately.

PER SERVING: 383 Kcals / 16.9g fat / 3.9g sat fat / 37.1g carbs / 1.9g sugar / 18g fibre / 22g protein / 2.6g salt

Kale & Butter Bean Casserole

Served bubbling hot, this filling casserole of nourishing, nutrient-packed butter beans, onions, tomatoes and kale, finished with a flurry of diced avocado, creates a really wholesome meal, perfect for a chilly winter's day.

Serves 6
Prep: 25 minutes, plus overnight soaking
Cook: 1¾–2 hours

350 g/12 oz butter beans, soaked overnight
1 tbsp cumin seeds
2 tsp dried oregano
3 tbsp groundnut oil
2 onions, chopped
2 garlic cloves, thinly sliced
1–3 fresh red or green chillies, deseeded and sliced
400 g/14 oz canned chopped tomatoes
450 ml/15 fl oz vegetable stock
175 g/6 oz shredded kale
5 tbsp chopped fresh coriander
juice of 1 lime
salt and pepper, optional
2 avocados, cubed and tossed with 1 tsp lime juice, to garnish
½ red onion, sliced, to garnish

1. Drain the beans, put them into a large saucepan and cover with water. Bring to the boil, boil for 15 minutes, then simmer for 30–45 minutes, until tender but not disintegrating. Drain and set aside.

2. Put the cumin seeds into a small dry frying pan over a medium heat and fry until fragrant. Add the oregano, fry for a few seconds, then immediately remove the mixture from the pan.

3. Lightly crush the mixture in a mortar with a pestle.

4. Heat the oil in a large, flameproof casserole over a medium heat. Add the chopped onions and the spice and herb mixture. Fry for 5 minutes, until the onions are translucent. Add the garlic and chillies and fry for a further 2 minutes.

5. Stir the tomatoes, beans and stock into the casserole. Season with salt and pepper, if using, and bring to the boil. Reduce the heat, cover and simmer for 30 minutes, stirring occasionally.

6. Increase the heat and stir in the kale. Simmer, uncovered, for 7 minutes, or until tender but still brightly coloured. Stir in the coriander and lime juice.

7. Ladle into soup bowls, garnish with the avocado and red onion and serve immediately.

PER SERVING: *400 Kcals / 15.8g fat / 2.7g sat fat / 52.5g carbs / 6.9g sugar / 14.4g fibre / 17.8g protein / 0.8g salt*

Beetroot Burgers in Buns

Makes 5

Prep: 30 minutes,
  plus standing and chilling
Cook: 35–40 minutes

100 g/3½ oz millet,
  rinsed and drained
175 ml/6 fl oz water
1 large raw beetroot (approximately
  150 g/5½ oz), grated
30 g/1 oz carrots, grated
175 g/6 oz courgettes, grated
60 g/2¼ oz walnuts, finely chopped
2 tbsp cider vinegar
2 tbsp olive oil
1 egg, beaten
2 tbsp cornflour
2 tbsp olive oil, for frying
salt and pepper, optional
5 multi-grain buns, split, to serve
5 lettuce leaves, to serve

Yogurt sauce

225 g/8 oz natural yogurt
2 garlic cloves, finely chopped

Wow your taste buds with these tasty griddled millet and mixed vegetable burgers. Stuffed into multigrain buns and served with a low-fat garlic yogurt sauce, they make an excellent lunch or supper dish for sharing.

1. Put the millet, water and salt, if using, in a small saucepan. Bring to a simmer over a medium heat, then reduce the heat to low, cover and cook for 20–25 minutes, or until tender. Remove from the heat and leave to stand for 5 minutes, covered with a lid.

2. Place the beetroot, carrots, courgettes and walnuts in a large bowl. Add the millet, vinegar, oil, and salt and pepper, if using, and mix well to combine. Add the egg and cornflour, mix again, then cover and chill in the refrigerator for 2 hours.

3. Meanwhile, to make the yogurt sauce, put the yogurt in a fine sieve over a bowl and leave to drain for at least 30 minutes. Stir in the garlic and season with salt and pepper, if using.

4. Spoon the beetroot mixture into five mounds on a chopping board, then squeeze them into patties using wet hands. Place a ridged griddle pan or large frying pan over a medium heat and coat with olive oil. Add the patties and cook for 10 minutes, or until browned, turning halfway through.

5. Top the base of each bun with a spoonful of the yogurt sauce. Place the burgers on top, then the lettuce, then the bun lid. Serve immediately.

PER BURGER IN BUN: *498 Kcals / 24.6g fat / 4.2g sat fat / 55g carbs / 9.6g sugar / 8.5g fibre / 16g protein / 0.8g salt*

181

Pumpkin, Feta & Aduki Bean Parcels

Served crisp, golden and freshly baked from the oven, these fantastic feta, bean and pumpkin-packed filo parcels provide a wholesome, meat-free lunch or supper for all the family to enjoy.

Serves 6

Prep: 40 minutes
Cook: 45–50 minutes

500 g/1 lb 2 oz pumpkin, cut into 2-cm/¾-inch cubes
4 shallots, quartered
1 tsp smoked paprika
1 tbsp olive oil
200 g/7 oz canned aduki beans, drained and rinsed
2 tbsp roughly chopped parsley
zest of 1 lemon
100 g/3½ oz feta cheese, crumbled
3 sheets of filo, each measuring 40 x 30 cm/16 x 12 inches
50 g/1¾ oz butter, melted
pepper, optional
1 tbsp snipped watercress, to garnish
green salad, to serve, optional

1. Preheat the oven to 200°C/400°F/Gas Mark 6. Place the pumpkin and shallots into a shallow roasting tin in an even layer and sprinkle with the paprika. Drizzle over the olive oil and mix well. Roast in the preheated oven for 20–25 minutes, or until the pumpkin is slightly golden and soft. Leave the oven on.

2. Place the pumpkin mixture into a large bowl. Using a potato masher, mash until the cubes have broken down. Stir in the aduki beans, parsley, lemon zest and feta cheese. Mix until all the ingredients are well combined. Season with pepper, if using.

3. Cut a filo sheet in half to create two long lengths of pastry (approximately 40 x 15 cm/16 x 6 inch) and brush one pastry length all over with melted butter. Cover the remaining pastry with a damp tea towel to keep it fresh.

4. Spoon a sixth of the pumpkin mixture on one end of the pastry length. Fold this edge up to meet one side to start the shape of a triangle. Fold the bottom point of the pastry up, sealing in the filling then complete the triangle by folding again in the opposite direction. Keep folding until you reach the top and lightly brush with a little more melted butter. Repeat with the other sheets of filo until you have six triangles.

5. Place the parcels on a baking tray and cook for 25 minutes, or until golden. Garnish with watercress and serve immediately, with a green salad, if desired.

PER SERVING: 213 Kcals / 13.4g fat / 7.3g sat fat / 18.4g carbs / 2.6g sugar / 1.9g fibre / 6g protein / 0.7g salt

Miso & Tofu Salad

This tempting salad of grilled sesame-sprinkled tofu, paired with nourishing green vegetables for vitality, boasts a fusion of fresh flavours from afar and creates an appealing meat-free meal for friends.

Serves 4
Prep: 25 minutes
Cook: 8–10 minutes

400 g/14 oz firm tofu, drained and cut into 1-cm/½-inch slices

1 tbsp sesame seeds

85 g/3 oz mangetout, thinly sliced

115 g/4 oz ready-to-eat beansprouts

150 g/5½ oz asparagus, trimmed and cut into long, thin slices

1 courgette, cut into matchsticks

1 Little Gem lettuce, leaves separated and cut into long slices

25 g/1 oz fresh coriander, roughly chopped

85 g/3 oz mixed ready-to-eat sprouting seeds, such as alfalfa and radish sprouts

Dressing
3 tbsp rice wine vinegar

2 tbsp soy sauce

3 tbsp sunflower oil

1 tbsp sweet white miso

2 garlic cloves, finely chopped

1. To make the dressing, put the vinegar and soy sauce in a jam jar, then add the oil, miso and garlic. Screw on the lid and shake well.

2. Preheat the grill to high and line the grill pan with foil. Put the tofu on the foil in a single layer. Mark criss-cross lines over each slice using a knife, then sprinkle with the sesame seeds. Spoon over half of the dressing, then grill for 8–10 minutes, turning once, until browned.

3. Put the mangetout, beansprouts, asparagus, courgette and lettuce on a platter. Pour over the remaining dressing and toss gently together. Sprinkle over the coriander and sprouts, then top with the hot tofu, drizzle with any pan juices and serve immediately.

PER SERVING: 236 Kcals / 15g fat / 1.7g sat fat / 15.4g carbs / 8.4g sugar / 4.8g fibre / 13.2g protein / 1.6g salt

Stuffed Red Peppers

Savour the fine flavour of these vibrant red vitamin-packed peppers, stuffed with an energy-giving medley of lean minced beef, assorted pulses, vegetables and spices. Perfect for a sustaining weekend meal.

Serves 4
Prep: 25 minutes
Cook: 1 hour

4 large red peppers, stalks left on, halved
    lengthways and deseeded
1 tbsp olive oil
1 red onion, finely chopped
400 g/14 oz lean minced beef
2 garlic cloves, finely chopped
¼ tsp smoked hot paprika or chilli powder
1 tsp ground cumin
400 g/14 oz canned chickpeas, drained and rinsed
400 g/14 oz canned green lentils, drained and rinsed
400 g/14 oz canned chopped tomatoes
125 ml/4 fl oz beef stock
salt and pepper, optional
175 g/6 oz low-fat Greek-style natural yogurt, optional
15 g/½ oz fresh mint, roughly chopped
15 g/½ oz fresh flat-leaf parsley, roughly chopped

1. Preheat the oven to 180°C/350°F/Gas Mark 4. Arrange the peppers cut-side up in a roasting tin.

2. Heat the oil in a frying pan over a medium heat. Add the red onion, minced beef and garlic and cook, stirring and breaking up the mince, for 5 minutes, or until evenly browned.

3. Stir in the paprika and cumin, then the chickpeas, lentils, tomatoes and stock. Season with salt and pepper, if using, then increase the heat to high and bring to the boil. Remove from the heat.

4. Spoon the mince mixture into the peppers, cover the dish with foil, then bake for 50 minutes, or until the peppers are tender and the mince is cooked.

5. Remove the foil, top each pepper with a spoonful of yogurt, if using, then sprinkle generously with the mint and parsley and serve immediately.

PER SERVING: 385 Kcals / 10.8g fat / 3g sat fat / 35g carbs / 14.3g sugar / 10.7g fibre / 32.5g protein / 0.5g salt

Spanish Vegetable Stew

Serves 4
Prep: 25 minutes
Cook: 55 minutes

2 tbsp virgin olive oil

1 onion, roughly chopped

1 aubergine, roughly chopped

½ tsp smoked hot paprika

2 garlic cloves, finely chopped

1 large red pepper, deseeded
and roughly chopped

250 g/9 oz baby new potatoes,
unpeeled and any larger ones halved

450 g/1 lb plum tomatoes, peeled and
roughly chopped

400 g/14 oz canned haricot beans
in water, drained and rinsed

150 ml/5 fl oz vegetable stock

2 sprigs of fresh rosemary

2 courgettes, roughly chopped

salt and pepper, optional

This wholesome and hearty Spanish stew is crammed with nutrient-dense vegetables and beans and fully flavoured with warming smoked paprika and robust rosemary. Serve on its own or with crusty bread for a satisfying meal.

1. Preheat the oven to 200°C/400°F/ Gas Mark 6. Heat 1 tablespoon of oil in a saucepan over a medium heat. Add the onion and fry for 5 minutes, or until softened. Add another tablespoon of oil, then add the aubergine, and fry, stirring, for 5 minutes, or until just beginning to soften and brown.

2. Stir in the smoked paprika and garlic, then the red pepper, potatoes and tomatoes. Add the haricot beans, stock and rosemary, then season with salt and pepper, if using. Bring to the boil, cover, turn the heat down to medium–low and simmer for 30 minutes, stirring from time to time.

3. Stir the courgettes into the stew, then cook, uncovered, for 10 minutes, or until all the vegetables are tender and the sauce has reduced slightly.

4. Ladle the stew into shallow bowls, discard the rosemary sprigs and serve immediately.

PER SERVING: *278 Kcals / 8.5g fat / 1.3g sat fat / 41.8g carbs / 13g sugar / 14.9g fibre / 10.4g protein / 0.4g salt*

Roasted Beetroot & Squash Salad

Raid the veggie box to make this scrumptious salad. Low-fat and loaded with vitamins, minerals and antioxidants, beetroot and butternut squash add vitality and plenty of feel-good factor to this sustaining mixed grain salad.

Serves 4
Prep: 25 minutes
Cook: 30 minutes

450 g/1 lb raw beetroot, green stalk trimmed,
   peeled and cut into 2-cm/¾-inch cubes
450 g/1 lb butternut squash flesh, cut into 2-cm/¾-inch cubes
4 tbsp olive oil
100 g/3½ oz brown basmati rice
100 g/3½ oz red Camargue rice
100 g/3½ oz quick-cook farro
115 g/4 oz beetroot leaves
salt and pepper, optional

Dressing
1 tbsp flaxseed oil
2 tbsp red wine vinegar
½ tsp smoked hot paprika
1 tsp fennel seeds, roughly crushed
2 tsp tomato purée

1. Preheat the oven to 200°C/400°F/Gas Mark 6. Put the beetroot and squash in a roasting tin, drizzle with half of the olive oil and season with salt and pepper, if using. Roast for 30 minutes, or until just tender.

2. Meanwhile, put the basmati and red Camargue rice in a saucepan of boiling water. Bring back to the boil, then simmer, uncovered, for 15 minutes. Add the farro and cook for 10 minutes more, or until all the grains are tender. Drain and rinse, then transfer to a platter.

3. To make the dressing, put all the ingredients and the remaining 2 tablespoons of olive oil in a jam jar. Season with salt and pepper, if using, screw on the lid and shake well. Drizzle the dressing over the rice mixture, then toss gently together.

4. Spoon the roasted vegetables over the grains and leave to cool. Toss gently together then sprinkle with the beetroot leaves and serve immediately.

PER SERVING: *528 Kcals / 19.2g fat / 2.5g sat fat / 64.9g carbs / 10.9g sugar / 10.1g fibre / 10.7g protein / 0.4g salt*

Mushroom Farro Risotto

Hearty wholegrain farro adds a delicious nutty flavour to this top-notch mushroom risotto. Flavoured with garlic, shallots and aromatic thyme, plus a handful of superfood spinach leaves, it provides a filling and nutritious meat-free meal.

Serves 4

Prep: 25 minutes
Cook: 50–55 minutes

175 g/6 oz farro
2 tbsp olive oil
250 g/9 oz chestnut mushrooms
5 shallots, finely chopped
4 garlic cloves, sliced
2 tbsp fresh thyme leaves
750 ml/1¼ pints vegetable stock
70 g/2½ oz baby spinach
25 g/1 oz grated Parmesan cheese
pepper, optional
2 tbsp roughly chopped fresh flat-leaf parsley, to garnish
4 tbsp natural yogurt, to serve

1. Bring a large saucepan of water to the boil. Add the farro to the pan and simmer gently for 15 minutes, to begin the cooking process. Drain the farro and set aside.

2. Meanwhile add half of the olive oil to a large, deep frying pan. Add the mushrooms and fry for 2–3 minutes over a high heat, or until they have softened. Remove the mushrooms from the pan and set aside on a plate.

3. Add the remaining olive oil to the frying pan and, once hot, add the shallots, garlic and thyme. Reduce the heat to medium and continue to fry for a few minutes until the shallots have softened, but not coloured.

PER SERVING: 303 Kcals / 11.1g fat / 3g sat fat / 43.6g carbs / 3.6g sugar / 4.3g fibre / 10.7g protein / 2.1g salt

4. Stir the softened farro through the shallot mixture and pour over the stock, in thirds, stirring well after each addition. Leave to simmer on a low heat, stirring occasionally, for about 30–35 minutes, or until the farro is soft but still has a little bite in the centre and the liquid has all but disappeared. If the pan runs dry, add a little more water.

5. Once the farro is cooked, return the mushrooms to the pan with the spinach. Allow the spinach to wilt before stirring through the Parmesan. Season with pepper, if using. Serve in bowls, garnished with flat-leaf parsley and a dollop of natural yogurt.

Power-packed Protein

Spicy Steak with Roasted Squash

Lean and juicy high-protein fillet steaks are lightly griddled, then served with roasted vegetables and a pleasing piquant sauce to produce this tantalizing meal, excellent for a weekend supper with family or friends.

Serves 4
Prep: 25–30 minutes
Cook: 35–40 minutes, plus resting

Roasted vegetables
750 g/1 lb 10 oz butternut squash, cut into chunks
4 garlic cloves, finely chopped
4 large portobello mushrooms, cut into thick slices
15 g/½ oz fresh sage, leaves only, finely chopped
2 tbsp olive oil

Chimichurri sauce
30 g/1 oz fresh flat-leaf parsley
½ tsp dried oregano
2 garlic cloves
1 shallot, chopped
¼ tsp dried chilli flakes
grated zest and juice of ½ lemon
2 tbsp red wine vinegar
2 tbsp olive oil
2 tbsp cold water

Steaks
4 x 175 g/6 oz fillet steaks
1 tbsp olive oil, for brushing
1 tbsp olive oil, for drizzling
salt and pepper, optional

1. Preheat the oven to 200°C/400°F/Gas Mark 6. Place the squash, garlic, mushrooms and sage into a large roasting tin. Drizzle over the olive oil and mix well. Season with salt and pepper, if using, and roast in the preheated oven for 25–30 minutes, turning once halfway through the cooking time.

2. Meanwhile, make the sauce. Place all of the ingredients, except the water, into a bowl and blend using a hand-held blender or food processor. Carefully pour in the water, adding just enough to reach a spooning consistency. Set aside.

PER SERVING: *527 Kcals / 28.2g fat / 5.8g sat fat / 29.6g carbs / 6.2g sugar / 5g fibre / 44.2g protein / 0.3g salt*

3. Brush the steaks with the olive oil and season with salt and pepper, if using. Place a heavy frying pan or griddle over a high heat and once smoking, add the steaks and reduce the heat to medium–high. Cook for 2–3 minutes on each side for medium–rare, or cook to your taste. Remove the steaks from the pan and leave them to rest for a few minutes before serving.

4. Cut the steaks into thick slices and serve on top of the roasted vegetables. Drizzle over the chimichurri sauce and the olive oil.

Chicken & Giant Couscous Salad

Serves 4
Prep: 35 minutes
Cook: 35–40 minutes

175 g/6 oz giant wholewheat couscous
175 g/6 oz cooked beetroot,
    in natural juices (drained
    weight), drained and diced
1 small red onion, finely chopped
125 g/4½ oz cherry tomatoes, halved
1 pomegranate, halved and
    seeds removed and reserved
juice of 2 lemons
2 tbsp flaxseed oil
2 tbsp olive oil
4 tsp tomato purée
2 tbsp roughly chopped fresh mint
1 tsp black peppercorns,
    roughly crushed
500 g/1 lb 2 oz chicken
    breast mini fillets, sliced
salt and pepper, optional

Low in fat and cholesterol-free, wholewheat couscous provides a good source of fibre, so when it's combined with protein-packed chicken, plus nutrient-rich beetroot and pomegranate seeds, this salad bursts with natural goodness.

1. Put the couscous in a saucepan of boiling water. Bring back to the boil, then simmer for 6—8 minutes, or until just tender. Drain into a sieve, rinse with cold water, then transfer to a salad bowl. Add the beetroot, then the onion, tomatoes and pomegranate seeds.

2. To make the dressing, put the juice of 1 lemon, the flaxseed oil, half of the olive oil and half of the tomato purée in a jam jar. Season with salt and pepper, if using, screw on the lid and shake well. Drizzle over the salad, then sprinkle on the chopped mint and toss together.

3. Put the remaining lemon juice, olive oil and tomato purée and the crushed peppercorns in a clean plastic bag, twist and shake well. Add the chicken, seal, then shake until the chicken is evenly coated.

4. Preheat a ridged griddle pan over a high heat. Cook the chicken (in batches if necessary) in the hot pan for 10 minutes, turning once or twice, until cooked through. Cut through the middle of a slice to check that the meat is no longer pink and any juices run clear and are piping hot. Arrange over the salad and serve.

PER SERVING: 503 Kcals / 18.9g fat / 2.3g sat fat / 51.4g carbs / 10.2g sugar / 7.7g fibre / 36.2g protein / 0.4g salt

Roast Pork with Gingered Apples

Serves 4

Prep: 25 minutes, plus marinating
Cook: 55 minutes, plus resting

2 garlic cloves, crushed
4 tbsp red wine
2 tbsp soft brown sugar
1 tbsp soy sauce
1 tsp sesame oil
½ tsp ground cinnamon
¼ tsp ground cloves
1 star anise, broken into pieces
½ tsp pepper
350 g/12 oz pork fillet
400 g/14 oz cooked French beans,
   to serve

Gingered apples

4 cooking apples, roughly chopped
1 tbsp rice vinegar
1 tbsp soft brown sugar
4 tbsp apple juice
1 tbsp finely chopped fresh ginger

Marinated lean roast pork fillet, accompanied by a home-made apple sauce with a ginger twist, creates this very appealing meal. Along with its warm, spicy flavour, fresh ginger is also a helpful digestive aid.

1. In a large bowl, combine the garlic, wine, brown sugar, soy sauce, sesame oil, cinnamon, cloves, star anise and pepper. Add the pork and toss to coat. Cover and refrigerate overnight.

2. Preheat the oven to 190°C/375°F/ Gas Mark 5. Heat a non-stick frying pan over a high heat. Remove the pork from the marinade and sear in the hot pan. Cook for about 8 minutes, or until browned on all sides. Transfer the pork to an ovenproof dish and drizzle with half of the marinade. Roast in the preheated oven for 15 minutes.

3. Turn the meat, drizzle the remaining marinade over the top and roast for 30 minutes, or until cooked through (insert a skewer into the centre of the meat and check that there is no pink meat).

4. Meanwhile, make the gingered apples. In a saucepan, combine all the ingredients and cook over a medium–high heat, until the liquid begins to boil. Reduce the heat to medium–low and simmer, stirring occasionally, for about 20 minutes, or until the apples are soft.

5. Remove the pork from the oven and set aside to rest for 5 minutes. Slice the meat and serve with the apples and French beans.

Tuna with Pak Choi & Soba Noodles

Top-notch tuna steaks team up with vitamin-rich pak choi and buckwheat soba noodles to make this revitalizing Japanese-style dish for two that is full of fresh, natural flavours and appeal.

Serves 2

Prep: 20–25 minutes
Cook: 20 minutes

400 g/14 oz pak choi

115 g/4 oz soba noodles

2 tuna steaks, about 175 g/6 oz each and 15 mm/½ inch thick

1 tbsp groundnut oil, for brushing

2 tbsp groundnut oil

2 slices fresh ginger, cut into matchsticks

½–1 fresh red chilli, deseeded and thinly sliced

4 spring onions, some green included, thickly sliced diagonally

140 g/5 oz frozen soya beans, thawed

2 tbsp chicken stock

squeeze of lime juice

3 tbsp chopped fresh coriander

salt and pepper, optional

1. Slice the pak choi stems into bite-sized pieces. Slice the leaves into broad ribbons.

2. Bring a large saucepan of water to the boil. Add the noodles, bring back to the boil and cook for 5–6 minutes, or until just tender. Drain, reserving the cooking water. Rinse the noodles well and set aside. Return the reserved water to the pan and keep warm over a low heat.

3. Meanwhile, cut the tuna steaks into thirds. Brush with oil and season with salt and pepper, if using. Heat a ridged griddle pan over a high heat. Add the tuna and fry for 2–2½ minutes on each side. Transfer to a plate and set aside in a warm place.

4. Heat a wok over a medium–high heat. Add the oil and sizzle the ginger, chilli and spring onions for a few seconds.

5. Add the pak choi stalks, soya beans and stock and stir-fry for 3 minutes. Add the pak choi leaves and stir-fry for a further minute. Add the lime juice and coriander, then season to taste with salt and pepper, if using.

6. Reheat the noodles in the cooking water, then drain thoroughly. Divide the noodles between two plates, add the vegetables and arrange the tuna on top. Serve immediately.

Squid with Saffron Aioli

Serves 2

Prep: 30–35 minutes,
  plus soaking and chilling
Cook: 14–16 minutes

500 g/1 lb 2 oz whole small squid,
  skinned, cleaned and gutted
3 tbsp cornflour
vegetable oil, for deep-frying
salt and pepper, optional
2 lemon wedges, to serve, optional

Aioli

small pinch of saffron strands
1 tsp lukewarm water
3 tbsp whole egg mayonnaise
½ small garlic clove, finely chopped

Salad

head of red chicory, leaves separated
25 g/1 oz watercress
10 g/¼ oz Parmesan cheese, shaved
juice of ¼ lemon
1 tbsp extra virgin olive oil

Fresh squid provides a rich source of protein and a good dose of vitamins and minerals. Deep-fried, then served with aioli and a simple salad, this decadent dish creates a mouthwatering meal for two.

1. To make the aioli, put the saffron and water in a small bowl and leave for 5 minutes. Stir during the soaking to release the flavour. Meanwhile, put the mayonnaise and garlic in a bowl and mix well. When the saffron has turned the water vibrant yellow, discard the saffron strands and stir the liquid into the mayonnaise. Transfer to two dipping bowls, cover with clingfilm and chill in the refrigerator.

2. To make the salad, put the chicory and watercress in a large bowl, then scatter over the cheese. Put the lemon juice and oil in a small jug and mix well with a fork.

3. Slice the squid body into 1-cm/ ½-inch rounds and cut the tentacles in half. Wash under the cold tap, then dry on kitchen paper. Put the cornflour on a plate, season with salt and pepper, if using, and toss the squid lightly in the mixture until thoroughly coated.

4. Heat the oil in a deep heavy-based saucepan, being careful not to fill the pan too high. To test whether it is hot enough, drop in a small cube of bread. If it takes about 30 seconds to turn golden, the oil is ready.

5. Cook the squid in two batches, as too much squid in the pan will make the oil temperature drop. Scatter half the squid in the oil and cook for 2–3 minutes, until the coating is just tinged a golden colour.

6. Using a slotted spoon, transfer the cooked squid to kitchen paper to drain, then keep warm in the oven while you cook the second batch.

7. Season the squid with salt and pepper, if using. Pour the dressing over the salad. Serve the squid immediately with the salad and aioli, and lemon wedges for squeezing over, if using.

Spiced Turkey Stew with Couscous

Just right for a chilly winter's day, recharge your batteries with this warming, wholesome stew of lean turkey and vibrant red antioxidant-rich vegetables, served with wholegrain couscous and scattered with fresh garden herbs.

Serves 4
Prep: 25 minutes
Cook: 25 minutes

1 tbsp virgin olive oil
500 g/1 lb 2 oz skinless and boneless turkey breasts,
   cut into 1.5-cm/¾-inch pieces
1 onion, roughly chopped
2 garlic cloves, finely chopped
1 red and 1 orange pepper, deseeded and roughly chopped
500 g/1 lb 2 oz tomatoes, roughly chopped
1 tsp cumin seeds, roughly crushed
1 tsp paprika
finely grated zest and juice of 1 lemon
salt and pepper, optional

To serve
200 g/7 oz wholegrain giant couscous
2 tbsp roughly chopped fresh flat-leaf parsley
2 tbsp roughly chopped fresh coriander

1. Heat the oil in a large frying pan over a medium heat. Add the turkey, a few pieces at a time, then add the onion. Fry, stirring, for 5 minutes, or until the turkey has turned golden.

2. Add the garlic, red and orange peppers and tomatoes, then stir in the cumin seeds and paprika. Add the lemon juice and season with salt and pepper, if using. Stir well, then cover and cook, stirring from time to time, for 20 minutes, or until the tomatoes have formed a thick sauce and the turkey is cooked through and the juices run clear with no sign of pink when a piece is cut in half.

3. Meanwhile, half-fill a saucepan with water and bring to the boil. Add the couscous and cook according to the packet instructions, or until just tender. Tip into a sieve and drain well.

4. Spoon the couscous onto plates and top with the turkey stew. Mix the parsley and coriander with the lemon zest, then sprinkle over the stew and serve.

PER SERVING: *433 Kcals / 6.6g fat / 0.8g sat fat / 55.5g carbs / 8.4g sugar / 9.1g fibre / 41.9g protein / 0.2g salt*

Gingered Salmon with Stir-fried Kale

Kale, the ultimate super leaf, contains high levels of vitamins, especially vitamin C, and when paired with super nutritious salmon steaks and broccoli, it creates a delicious dish that is brimming with beneficial nutrients.

Serves 4
Prep: 20 minutes
Cook: 10 minutes

4 x 150 g/5½ oz salmon steaks, skinned
5-cm/2-inch piece fresh ginger,
   finely chopped
3 garlic cloves, finely chopped
1 red chilli, deseeded and finely chopped
3 tbsp soy sauce
200 g/7 oz broccoli, cut into florets
6 tbsp water
1 tbsp sunflower oil
1 large leek, sliced
115 g/4 oz kale, thinly shredded
2 tbsp Shaoxing wine
juice of 1 orange

1. Preheat the grill to medium–high and line the base of the grill pan with foil. Arrange the salmon on the grill pan and fold up the edges of the foil to make a dish. Sprinkle over half of the ginger, half of the garlic and half of the chilli, then drizzle with 1 tablespoon of soy sauce. Grill, turning once, for 8–10 minutes, or until browned and the fish flakes easily when pressed with a knife.

2. Meanwhile, put the broccoli and water in a wok or large frying pan, cover and cook over a medium–high heat for 3–4 minutes, or until the broccoli is almost tender. Pour off any remaining water.

3. Add the oil to the wok and increase the heat to high. When it is hot, add the leek, kale and the remaining ginger, garlic and chilli and stir-fry for 2–3 minutes, or until the kale has just wilted.

4. Mix in the remaining soy sauce, the Shaoxing wine and orange juice and cook for 1 minute more. Spoon onto plates, break up a salmon steak over each plate and serve immediately.

PER SERVING: 416 Kcals / 24.1g fat / 5g sat fat / 15.3g carbs / 5.1g sugar / 2.7g fibre / 34.6g protein / 1.9g salt

Pork-stuffed Cabbage Leaves

Serves 4
Prep: 25 minutes
Cook: 1 hour

1 tbsp olive oil
15 g/½ oz butter
400 g/14 oz canned
   chopped tomatoes
425 ml/15 fl oz chicken stock
1 onion, grated
8 large cabbage leaves,
   thick stalks removed
300 g/10½ oz fresh pork mince
100 g/3½ oz freshly cooked
   white rice
finely grated zest of 1 lemon
2 tsp paprika
½ tsp dill seeds or caraway seeds
1 egg, lightly beaten
salt and pepper, optional
2 tbsp chopped fresh dill, to garnish

Paprika and dill or caraway seeds impart a lovely flavour to protein-rich lean minced pork to make the tasty filling for these stuffed cabbage leaves. Serve with warm crusty bread for a fabulous supper.

1. Heat the oil and butter in a large frying pan. Add the tomatoes, stock and all but 2 tablespoons of the grated onion. Season with salt and pepper, if using. Bring to the boil, then reduce the heat and simmer gently while you prepare the cabbage leaves.

2. Bring a large saucepan of water to the boil. Add the cabbage leaves and blanch for 2 minutes. Drain and rinse under cold running water, then pat dry.

3. Combine the pork, rice, lemon zest, paprika, dill seeds, egg and the remaining onion. Add salt and pepper, if using, and mix well. Divide the stuffing between the cabbage leaves. Fold over the base and sides of each leaf, then roll up to make a parcel.

4. Place the parcels seam-side down in the sauce. Cover and simmer over a low heat for 45 minutes, or until cooked through.

5. Sprinkle with fresh dill and serve immediately.

PER SERVING: _369 Kcals / 24.8g fat / 9g sat fat / 19.7g carbs / 6.6g sugar / 4g fibre / 18.3g protein / 1.2g salt_

Slow-cooked Beef with Smashed Butter Beans

A warming and restorative casserole combining succulent shreds of fall-apart beef in a flavourful stock is served with spoonfuls of herb and garlic-seasoned butter beans, making it ideal for keeping those wintry chills at bay.

Serves 6

Prep: 30 minutes
Cook: 4¼–4¾ hours

2 tbsp olive oil
1.6 kg/3 lb 8 oz beef brisket
4 onions, sliced
2 garlic cloves, crushed
1 tbsp tomato purée
1 kg/2 lb 4 oz ripe tomatoes, cut into quarters
750 ml/1¼ pints beef stock
salt and pepper, optional
2 tbsp roughly chopped fresh parsley, to garnish

Smashed butter beans

1 tbsp olive oil
3 shallots, finely chopped
3 garlic cloves, finely sliced
1 fresh rosemary sprig, finely chopped
800 g/1 lb 12 oz canned butter beans, drained and rinsed
juice and zest of 1 lemon
salt and pepper, optional

1. Place a 6-litre/10½-pint flameproof casserole dish over a high heat. Add the olive oil and, using tongs to hold the meat, brown the beef all over. Set the beef aside. Reduce the heat slightly and add the onions and garlic. Cook for 4–5 minutes, or until the onion and garlic have softened. Stir in the tomato purée. Add the fresh tomatoes and continue to cook for 1–2 minutes.

2. Return the beef to the dish and nestle the beef in the centre of the pot. Pour the hot stock around the beef. Season with salt and pepper, if using.

3. Reduce the heat to low. Partially cover the dish, allowing just a little steam to escape, and cook for 4–4 ½ hours, stirring regularly to prevent the bottom of the saucepan sticking. Top up with a little cold water if you think the pot is looking dry. The beef should be tender and easily tear apart.

4. Meanwhile, to make the smashed butter beans, heat the oil in a large frying pan and fry the shallots, garlic and rosemary for 3–4 minutes, or until the shallots are soft. Stir in the drained butter beans with 200 ml/7 fl oz water. Bring to a gentle simmer and cook for 5 minutes, or until the butter beans are softened. Gently mash the butter beans, stirring through the juice and zest of the lemon. Season with salt and pepper, if using.

5. Serve the slow-cooked beef on top of a spoonful of smashed butter beans in six dishes. Garnish with the chopped parsley.

PER SERVING: *668 Kcals / 33.1g fat / 11g sat fat / 30.4g carbs / 9.2g sugar / 7.9g fibre / 62.9g protein / 1.8g salt*

Jerk Chicken with Papaya & Avocado Salsa

Serves 4
Prep: 35 minutes
Cook: 30–35 minutes

1 kg/2 lb 4 oz small chicken
   drumsticks, skinned
1 tbsp olive oil
1 cos lettuce, leaves separated
   and torn into pieces, optional
85 g/3 oz baby spinach, optional

Jerk spice rub
1 tsp allspice berries, crushed
1 tsp coriander seeds, crushed
1 tsp mild paprika
¼ tsp freshly grated nutmeg
1 tbsp fresh thyme leaves
1 tbsp black peppercorns,
   coarsely crushed
pinch of salt

Papaya & avocado salsa
1 papaya, halved, deseeded,
   peeled and cut into cubes
2 large avocados, stoned,
   peeled and cut into cubes
finely grated zest and juice of 1 lime
½ red chilli, deseeded and
   finely chopped
½ red onion, finely chopped
15 g/½ oz fresh coriander,
   finely chopped
2 tsp chia seeds

Stimulate your senses with these sizzling spicy chicken legs, accompanied by a nutrient-rich fruit salsa and finished with a sprinkling of chia seeds. This makes a great gluten-free and dairy-free meal for sharing.

1. Preheat the oven to 200°C/400°F/ Gas Mark 6. To make the jerk spice rub, mix together all the ingredients in a small bowl.

2. Slash each chicken drumstick two or three times with a knife, then put them in a roasting tin and drizzle with the oil. Sprinkle the spice mix over the chicken, then rub it in with your fingers, washing your hands well afterwards.

3. Roast the chicken for 30–35 minutes, or until browned with piping hot juices that run clear with no sign of pink when a knife is inserted into the thickest part of a drumstick.

4. Meanwhile, to make the salsa, put the papaya and avocados in a bowl, sprinkle over the lime zest and juice, then toss well. Add the chilli, red onion, coriander and chia seeds and stir.

5. Toss the lettuce and spinach together, if using. Serve with the chicken and salsa.

Scallops with Pea Purée

Serves 4
Prep: 25 minutes
Cook: 12–14 minutes

500 g/1 lb 2 oz frozen peas
30 g/1 oz fresh mint leaves,
   roughly chopped
150 g/5½ oz butter
12 fat scallops, roes attached, if
   possible, and removed from
   their shells
salt and pepper, optional

Frozen peas and fresh scallops together pack a powerful protein punch in this tempting light lunch or supper.

1. Bring a large saucepan of water to the boil, then add the peas. Bring back to the boil and simmer for 3 minutes. Drain the peas, then put them in a food processor or blender with the mint, 100 g/3½ oz of the butter and salt, if using.

2. Process to a smooth purée, adding a little hot water if the mixture needs loosening. Cover and keep warm.

3. Pat the scallops dry, then season with salt and pepper, if using. Place a large frying pan over a high heat and add the remaining butter. When the butter starts to smoke, add the scallops and sear them for 1–2 minutes on each side. They should be brown and crisp on the outside but light and moist in the middle. Remove the pan from the heat.

4. Spread a spoonful of pea purée on each of four plates and place three scallops on top of each. Serve immediately.

PER SERVING: 429 Kcals / 31.3g fat / 19.4g sat fat / 19.5g carbs / 8.1g sugar / 6.1g fibre / 19.8g protein / 1.3g salt

Lean Beef Stir-fry

Made in a matter of minutes, this sensational stir-fry is heaped with fresh, healthy ingredients and delivers perfectly on flavour, texture and appeal. Serve with cooked noodles or brown rice, if you like.

Serves 2
Prep: 20 minutes
Cook: 10 minutes

2 tsp olive oil

140 g/5 oz beef steak, such as topside, visible fat removed, cut into thin strips

1 orange pepper, deseeded and cut into thin strips

4 spring onions, finely chopped

1–2 fresh jalapeño chillies, deseeded and thinly sliced

2 garlic cloves, finely chopped

115 g/4 oz mangetout, halved diagonally

115 g/4 oz large field mushrooms, sliced

2 tsp hoisin sauce

1 tbsp orange juice

85 g/3 oz rocket or watercress

4 tbsp sweet chilli sauce, to serve, optional

1. Heat the oil in a wok over a medium–high heat for 30 seconds. Add the beef and stir-fry for 1 minute, or until browned. Transfer to a plate with a slotted spoon.

2. Add the orange pepper, spring onions, jalapeño chillies and garlic to the wok and stir-fry for 2 minutes. Add the mangetout and mushrooms and stir-fry for 2 minutes more.

3. Return the beef to the wok. Add the hoisin sauce and orange juice and stir-fry for 2–3 minutes, or until the beef is cooked and the vegetables are tender but still firm. Add the rocket and stir-fry until it starts to wilt. Serve immediately, with a small bowl of sweet chilli sauce, if using.

PER SERVING: *359 Kcals / 16.4g fat / 2.6g sat fat / 34.1g carbs / 24g sugar / 5.3g fibre / 21.9g protein / 1.4g salt*

Monkfish in Pesto & Parma Ham with Ricotta Spinach

Serves 4

Prep: 30–35 minutes
Cook: 25–30 minutes

8 Parma ham slices
3 tbsp fresh green pesto
8 large fresh basil leaves
600 g/1 lb 5 oz monkfish
    tail, separated into 2 fillets
1 tbsp olive oil

Ricotta spinach

2 tbsp olive oil
1 garlic clove, thinly sliced
150 g/5½ oz baby spinach
2 tbsp ricotta cheese
salt and pepper, optional

Tempt your guests to the table with this sensational Parma ham and pesto-wrapped monkfish, oven-roasted to perfection and served with vitamin C-rich spinach dotted with fresh ricotta. It's certain to impress!

1. Preheat the oven to 180°C/350°F/Gas Mark 4. Lay two large sheets of clingfilm side-by-side on a work surface. Arrange the ham slices on the clingfilm so they lay top to bottom and the slices overlap by 1 cm/½ inch. Spread the pesto all over the ham, leaving a 2-cm/¾-inch border around the edge. Scatter the basil over the top.

2. Put one monkfish fillet on top of the pesto and basil, then lay the other fillet next to it the other way round, so its thick end is against its neighbour's thin end.

3. Fold the ham over the ends of the fish and then, using the clingfilm, roll and encase the whole fillet tightly in the ham. Remove the clingfilm. Transfer to a roasting tin so the join in the ham is on the bottom, and lightly drizzle with the oil.

4. Roast in the preheated oven for 20–25 minutes, or until cooked through but still moist. Cover with kitchen foil to keep the fish warm.

5. To make the ricotta spinach, heat the oil in a large frying pan over a medium–high heat. Add the garlic and cook for 30 seconds, or until it is soft but not burnt. Stir in the spinach and cook, stirring all the time so the oil coats the leaves, for 1 minute, or until it is wilted but not completely collapsed. Transfer to a serving bowl, dot with blobs of the ricotta and season with salt and pepper, if using.

6. Place the fish on a serving platter, carve into slices and pour over any cooking juices from the roasting tin. Serve with the spinach.

PER SERVING: *372 Kcals* / *25.1g fat* / *5.7g sat fat* / *2.5g carbs* / *0.2g sugar* / *1.1g fibre* / *33.4g protein* / *1.6g salt*

223

Lamb & Spinach Meatballs

Serves 4
Prep: 25–30 minutes
Cook: 1 hour

Meatballs
500 g/1 lb 2 oz lean lamb mince
30 g/1 oz fresh breadcrumbs
70 g/2½ oz frozen chopped
   spinach, defrosted
1 tbsp dried oregano
1 tsp ground cumin
1 tbsp olive oil, for frying

Tomato sauce
4 shallots, finely chopped
4 garlic cloves, sliced
25 g/1 oz fresh basil, roughly chopped
1 tbsp tomato purée
800 g/1 lb 12 oz tomatoes, cores
   removed and roughly chopped
150 ml/5 fl oz vegetable stock
2 tbsp red wine vinegar

400 g/14 oz wholewheat spaghetti
salt and pepper, optional
1 tbsp chopped fresh basil, to garnish

Warming cumin and fragrant oregano add wonderful flavour to these succulent lamb and spinach meatballs. Served with a tasty tomato sauce and fibre-packed wholewheat spaghetti, this is sure to become a family favourite.

1. To make the meatballs, place the mince, breadcrumbs, spinach, oregano and cumin in a large bowl. Gently mix together using damp hands and divide the mixture into 12. Shape each portion into a round meatball.

2. Heat the olive oil in a deep frying pan over a medium–high heat. Add the meatballs in batches and fry for a few minutes, turning regularly, until browned all over. Remove from the pan and set aside.

3. To make the sauce, add the shallots and garlic to the pan and fry in the residual oil. Add a little more oil if needed and fry until the mixture is soft and beginning to caramelize. Reduce the heat to medium, stir in the basil and tomato purée and cook for a further minute. Stir in the chopped tomatoes and cook for 5–6 minutes, stirring until the tomatoes begin to break down.

4. Add the stock and red wine vinegar and simmer, uncovered, for 25 minutes, or until the sauce has broken down and started to thicken. Return the meatballs to the pan, cover and cook for 12–15 minutes. Season with salt and pepper, if using.

5. Meanwhile, cook the spaghetti in boiling water for 12–14 minutes, or until tender but still firm to the bite. Drain then divide between four bowls. Serve the meatballs and sauce over the spaghetti, garnished with fresh basil.

PER SERVING: 782 Kcals / 31g fat / 13.7g sat fat / 94.2g carbs / 11.2g sugar / 12g fibre / 39.9g protein / 0.7g salt

Warm Crab, Puy Lentil & Herb Salad

Tenderstem broccoli is an excellent source of vitamin C, and when teamed up with protein-rich lentils and crab, it creates a sensational super-charged salad ideal for a quick and easy mid-week supper for two.

Serves 2
Prep: 25 minutes
Cook: 35 minutes

200 g/7 oz tenderstem broccoli, any large stems cut in half
200 g/7 oz Puy lentils, cooked
zest of 1 large lemon
3 tbsp roughly chopped fresh parsley
2 tbsp roughly chopped fresh dill
40 g/1½ oz rocket
225 g/8 oz crab meat
1 tbsp roughly chopped fresh flat-leaf parsley, to garnish
1 tbsp roughly chopped fresh dill, to garnish
salt and pepper, optional

Dressing
juice of 1 large lemon
2 tbsp olive oil
3 tbsp natural yogurt
2–3 tbsp warm water

1. Bring a saucepan of water to the boil, reduce to a simmer and add the broccoli. Cook for 4–5 minutes, or until the broccoli is just tender. Drain immediately under cool running water and set aside.

2. In a large bowl, gently mix the cooked broccoli, Puy lentils, lemon zest, parsley and dill. Season with salt and pepper, if using.

3. To make the dressing, pour the lemon juice, olive oil and yogurt into an empty jar. Screw on the lid and shake vigorously. Loosen with a little warm water until you have the desired consistency.

4. Pour the dressing over the salad. Add the rocket and crab meat and mix together delicately, being careful not to bruise the salad leaves. Transfer the salad to a serving dish and garnish with the remaining dill and parsley. Serve immediately.

PER SERVING: 390 Kcals / 15.9g fat / 2.5g sat fat / 30.4g carbs / 5.6g sugar / 11.9g fibre / 34.3g protein / 2.4g salt

Chicken with Pomegranate & Beetroot Tabbouleh

Serves 4
Prep: 25–30 minutes
Cook: 35–45 minutes

225 g/8 oz wheatberries
4 raw beetroot (approximately
   350 g/12 oz), cut into cubes
500 g/1 lb 2 oz skinless and boneless
   chicken breasts, thinly sliced
1 small red onion, thinly sliced
200 g/7 oz cherry tomatoes, halved
seeds of 1 small pomegranate
2 tbsp roughly chopped fresh mint
70 g/2½ oz baby spinach
salt and pepper, optional

Dressing
juice of 1 lemon
4 tbsp virgin olive oil
2 garlic cloves, finely chopped
1 tsp light muscovado sugar

Heaped with feel-good ingredients, beetroot and pomegranate seeds, along with high-protein chicken, create this wholesome tabbouleh.

1. Half-fill the base of a steamer with water, bring to the boil, then add the wheatberries to the water. Put the beetroot in the steamer top, cover with a lid and steam for 20–25 minutes, or until the wheatberries and beetroot are cooked. Drain the wheatberries.

2. Meanwhile, to make the dressing, put the lemon juice, oil, garlic and sugar in a jam jar. Season with salt and pepper, if using, then screw on the lid and shake well.

3. Put the chicken in a bowl, add half of the dressing and toss well. Preheat a griddle pan over a medium–high heat. Add the chicken and cook, turning once or twice, for 8–10 minutes, or until golden and cooked through. Cut one of the larger slices of chicken in half to check that the meat is no longer pink and that the juices run clear.

4. Put the red onion, tomatoes and pomegranate seeds in a large shallow bowl. Add the wheatberries, beetroot and mint. Divide the spinach between four plates, spoon the wheatberry mixture over them, then arrange the chicken on top. Serve with the remaining dressing in a small jug.

PER SERVING: *562 Kcals / 18.1g fat / 2.6g sat fat / 64.9g carbs / 12.8g sugar / 13.4g fibre / 38.2g protein / 0.5g salt*

Tuna & Wasabi Burgers

Try this tantalizing new way with fresh tuna and cook up these healthy burgers. They're served on toasted ciabatta, topped with nutrient-rich peppery watercress, with Japanese-inspired pickled vegetables on the side.

Serves 4

Prep: 35 minutes, plus cooling, pickling and chilling
Cook: 20 minutes

Pickled vegetables

4 tbsp rice wine vinegar

1 tbsp soft light brown sugar

125 ml/4 fl oz water

½ tsp coriander seeds, crushed

½ tsp mustard seeds

½ cucumber, sliced

2 carrots, cut into matchsticks

6 radishes, thinly sliced

3 shallots, thinly sliced

Tuna burgers

450 g/1 lb tuna steaks

25 g /1 oz fresh coriander, finely chopped

zest and juice of 1 lime

2 tsp wasabi paste

4 spring onions, finely chopped

4 tbsp mayonnaise

4 wholemeal ciabatta slices

1 tbsp olive oil, for brushing

100 g/3½ oz watercress

1. To make the pickled vegetables, place the vinegar and sugar with the water in a small saucepan over a high heat. Bring to a gentle simmer and stir until the sugar dissolves. Remove from the heat and add the coriander and mustard seeds. Place the cucumber, carrots, radish and shallots into a small bowl or sterilized jar. Pour over the pickling liquid and leave to cool and pickle for 4 hours or overnight.

2. Slice the tuna steaks into 2.5 cm/1 inch pieces and briefly pulse in a food processor until just chopped. Transfer to a large bowl and combine with the coriander, lime zest and juice, wasabi paste, spring onions and 2 tablespoons of the mayonnaise. Mix well and place in a refrigerator for 15 minutes.

3. Meanwhile, preheat a griddle pan. Griddle the ciabatta slices until toasted and set aside.

4. Shape the tuna mixture into four burger shapes and brush each with oil. Griddle for 6 minutes on each side, or until the burgers are cooked through.

5. Serve the tuna burgers on the toasted ciabatta slices, topped with the remaining mayonnaise and the watercress and with the pickled vegetables on the side.

PER SERVING: 356 Kcals / 10.2g fat / 1.5g sat fat / 34.4g carbs / 10.4g sugar / 4.9g fibre / 32.4g protein / 1.1g salt

Pork Medallions with Pomegranate

Vitamin-loaded kale and fresh flat-leaf parsley add vivid green colour to this nourishing wheatberry and pan-fried pork platter, dotted with bright pink jewel-like pomegranate seeds for extra goodness and appeal.

Serves 4
Prep: 20 minutes
Cook: 40–45 minutes

150 g/5½ oz wheatberries
25 g/1 oz fresh flat-leaf parsley, roughly chopped
55 g/2 oz kale, thinly shredded
seeds of 1 pomegranate
1 tbsp olive oil
500 g/1 lb 2 oz pork medallions, visible fat removed
2 garlic cloves, finely chopped
salt and pepper, optional

Dressing
50 g/1¾ oz walnuts, roughly chopped
3 tbsp virgin olive oil
3 tsp pomegranate molasses
juice of 1 lemon

1. Bring a medium saucepan of water to the boil. Add the wheatberries and simmer for 25–30 minutes, or until tender. Drain and rinse.

2. Meanwhile, to make the dressing, put the walnuts in a large frying pan and toast for 2–3 minutes, or until just beginning to brown. Put the virgin olive oil, the pomegranate molasses and lemon juice in a small bowl and mix together with a fork. Season with salt and pepper, if using, and stir in the hot walnuts.

3. Mix together the parsley, kale and pomegranate seeds in a large bowl.

4. Heat the olive oil in the frying pan over a medium heat. Add the pork and garlic, season with salt and pepper, if using, and fry for 10 minutes, turning halfway through, until browned and cooked. Cut into the centre of one of the pork medallions; any juices that run out should be clear and piping hot with steam rising. Slice the pork into strips.

5. Add the wheatberries to the kale mixture and gently toss. Transfer to a platter, pour over the dressing, then top with the pork.

PER SERVING: 518 Kcals / 25.3g fat / 3.5g sat fat / 41.6g carbs / 5.2g sugar / 8.3g fibre / 34.3g protein / 0.8g salt

Country-style Ham & Pinto Beans

Pinto beans are an excellent low-fat source of protein, fibre and other essential nutrients and combine perfectly with fresh vegetables and cooked ham to make this satisfying, soul-warming supper dish.

Serves 4
Prep: 15–20 minutes
Cook: 1 hour

2 tbsp olive oil

1 large onion, chopped

2 green peppers, deseeded and chopped

4 garlic cloves, crushed

1 tsp ground cumin

500 g/1 lb 2 oz cooked pinto beans

3 tbsp tomato ketchup

25 g/1 oz soft dark brown sugar

2 tbsp cider vinegar

2 tsp Worcestershire sauce

2 tsp French mustard

150 ml/5 fl oz chicken stock

250 g/9 oz cubed cooked ham

salt and pepper, optional

2 tbsp chopped fresh flat-leaf parsley, to garnish

400 g/14 oz freshly cooked brown rice, to serve

1. Heat the oil in a flameproof casserole set over a medium–low heat. Add the onion and peppers and cook for 5 minutes, stirring occasionally. Add the garlic and cumin, stir to combine and cook for a further minute.

2. Add the beans, ketchup, sugar, vinegar, Worcestershire sauce, mustard, stock and ham, stirring to combine everything well. Bring to a simmer, cover with a lid and cook gently for 45 minutes.

3. Season with salt and pepper, if using, and sprinkle over the parsley. Serve with freshly cooked brown rice.

PER SERVING: *503 Kcals / 11.7g fat / 2.3g sat fat / 72.1g carbs / 12.9g sugar / 14.5g fibre / 29.6g protein / 2.3g salt*

Red Cabbage, Turkey & Quinoa Pilaf

Quinoa, which is a seed and not a grain, is a healthy low-carb alternative to rice and is high in protein too. It pairs up perfectly with red cabbage and low-fat turkey in this sustaining supper dish.

Serves 4

Prep: 25 minutes, plus standing
Cook: 50–55 minutes

90 g/3¼ oz white quinoa
90 g/3¼ oz red quinoa
4 tbsp vegetable oil
1 large red onion, halved and sliced
1 tsp cumin seeds, crushed
10-cm/4-inch cinnamon stick, broken
½ head of red cabbage, core removed, leaves sliced into ribbons
350 ml/12 fl oz chicken stock
350 g/12 oz cooked turkey, cut into bite-sized pieces
2 carrots, shaved into ribbons
85 g/3 oz dried cranberries
85 g/3 oz Brazil nuts, roughly chopped
salt and pepper, optional
2 tbsp fresh flat-leaf parsley leaves, to garnish

1. Combine the white quinoa and red quinoa, then place in a sieve and rinse under cold running water. Put in a saucepan with salt, if using, and enough water to cover by 15 mm/½ inch. Bring to the boil, cover and simmer over a very low heat for 15 minutes. Remove from the heat but leave the pan covered for 5 minutes to allow the grains to swell. Fluff up the grains with a fork and set aside.

2. Heat the oil in a large frying pan over a medium–high heat. Add the onion with the spices and fry for 5 minutes, or until the onion is soft but not coloured.

3. Add the cabbage, 250 ml/9 fl oz of the stock and season with salt and pepper, if using. Cover and cook over a medium heat for 15–20 minutes, until the cabbage is just tender. Add the turkey, carrots, cranberries and Brazil nuts. Fry, uncovered, for 5 minutes, until the turkey is heated through.

4. Gently stir in the cooked quinoa. Add the remaining stock and check the seasoning, if using. Cook for 2 minutes to heat through. Garnish with parsley and serve immediately.

PER SERVING: *688 Kcals / 32.2g fat / 6g sat fat / 67.3g carbs / 22.6g sugar / 11.1g fibre / 38.4g protein / 1g salt*

The Sweet Stuff

Healthy Apple Crumble

Serves 6

Prep: 25 minutes, plus cooling
Cook: 40–45 minutes

800 g/1 lb 12 oz cooking apples,
  peeled, cored and chopped
  into 2-cm/¾-inch chunks
pinch of ground cloves
pinch of ground cinnamon
1 tsp ground ginger
3 tbsp brown sugar

Topping

200 g/7 oz rolled oats
½ tsp ground cinnamon
3 tbsp runny honey
3 tbsp coconut oil, at room temperature
50 g/1¾ oz macadamia
  nuts, roughly chopped
2 tbsp demerara sugar

The sugar content of this fruity firm favourite has cleverly been cut but it still tastes just as good. Healthy wholegrain oats, macadamia nuts and coconut oil add extra goodness to the wholesome topping too.

1. Preheat the oven to 180°C/350°F/ Gas Mark 4.

2. Place the apple chunks in a large saucepan. Add 2 tablespoons of cold water, the cloves, cinnamon, ginger and brown sugar and place over a medium heat. Stew for about 15 minutes, stirring regularly, or until the apples begin to just lose their shape. Once mushy, put the apples into a 1.2 litre/2 pint baking dish.

3. To make the topping, simply place the oats in a medium bowl. Stir in the cinnamon, honey, coconut oil, macadamia nuts and sugar and mix well.

4. Sprinkle the topping mixture over the stewed apple and bake for 25–30 minutes, or until golden. Remove from the oven and leave to cool for a few minutes before serving.

PER SERVING: 378 Kcals / 15.4g fat / 7.3g sat fat / 59g carbs / 32.4g sugar / 5.7g fibre / 5.4g protein / trace salt

Green Tea Fruit Salad

Bursting with beneficial vitamins and antioxidants, this multi-coloured fruit salad provides a light and delicious dessert. Pistachios and pomegranate seeds add a final flourish of goodness too.

Serves 4
Prep: 25 minutes, plus brewing, cooling and chilling
Cook: No cooking

2 tsp green tea
225 ml/8 fl oz boiling water
1 tbsp runny honey
½ small watermelon, cut into cubes
1 large mango, cut into cubes
1 papaya, deseeded, cut into cubes
2 pears, cut into cubes
2 kiwi fruit, cut into cubes
2 tbsp roughly chopped fresh mint
seeds of ½ pomegranate
2 tbsp roughly chopped pistachio nuts

1. Place the tea into a jug or teapot, pour over the boiling water and leave to brew for 3–4 minutes. Strain into a small bowl, stir in the honey and leave to cool.

2. Put the watermelon, mango and papaya in a large serving bowl, then add the pears, kiwi fruit and mint. Pour over the cooled green tea and stir everything gently together.

3. Cover the fruit salad with clingfilm and chill in the refrigerator for 1 hour. Stir gently to mix the tea through the fruit.

4. Spoon the fruit salad into four bowls. Serve immediately, sprinkled with the pomegranate seeds and pistachio nuts.

PER SERVING: 258 Kcals / 3.5g fat / 0.4g sat fat / 59.5g carbs / 45.3g sugar / 8.4g fibre / 4.1g protein / trace salt

Coconut Milk, Strawberry & Honey Ice Cream

Serves 6

Prep: 30 minutes, plus freezing
Cook: No cooking

450 g/1 lb strawberries,
  hulled and halved
400 ml/14 fl oz canned
  full-fat coconut milk
85 g/3 oz runny honey
3 tbsp crushed hazelnuts, to serve

Fresh strawberries, heaped with healthy vitamin C, combine beautifully with coconut milk and healthful honey to produce a really sumptuous home-made ice cream. Crushed hazelnuts add a final feel-good crunch for serving.

1. Purée the strawberries in a food processor or liquidizer, then press through a sieve set over a mixing bowl to remove the seeds.

2. Add the coconut milk and honey to the strawberry purée and whisk together.

3. Pour the mixture into a large roasting tin until it is a depth of 2 cm/¾ inch. Cover the top of the tin with clingfilm, then freeze for about 2 hours until just set.

4. Scoop back into the food processor or liquidizer and blitz again until smooth to break down the ice crystals. Pour into a plastic container or 900-g/2-lb loaf tin lined with non-stick baking paper. Place the lid on the plastic container or fold the paper over the ice cream in the loaf tin. Return to the freezer for 3–4 hours, or until firm enough to scoop.

5. Serve immediately or leave in the freezer overnight or until needed. Thaw at room temperature for 15 minutes to soften slightly, then scoop into individual dishes and top with crushed hazelnuts to serve.

PER SERVING: *230 Kcals / 17.5g fat / 12.8g sat fat / 20.1g carbs / 17.1g sugar / 2g fibre / 2.6g protein / trace salt*

Black Bean & Date Brownies

Black beans and Medjool dates enrich these moreish brownies to create a tempting power snack that will do the trick when you need a chocolate hit or simply crave something sweet after a meal.

Makes 16

Prep: 25 minutes, plus cooling
Cook: 28 minutes, plus standing

100 g/3½ oz plain chocolate chips, 70% cocoa solids
3 tbsp coconut oil
375 g/13 oz black beans in water, drained and rinsed
175 g/6 oz Medjool dates, halved and stoned
3 eggs
70 g/2½ oz light muscovado sugar
1 tsp vanilla extract
55 g/2 oz cocoa powder
1½ tsp baking powder
½ tsp ground cinnamon
¼ tsp sea salt

1. Preheat the oven to 180°C/350°F/Gas Mark 4. Line a 20-cm/8-inch shallow square cake tin with a square of non-stick baking paper.

2. Add 55 g/2 oz of the chocolate chips to a small saucepan with the oil and heat over a very low heat until the oil has melted. Remove from the heat and leave to stand for a few minutes until the chocolate has melted completely.

3. Meanwhile, add the beans and dates to a food processor or blender and process to a coarse purée. Add the eggs, sugar, vanilla extract, chocolate and coconut oil mixture, and process again until smooth.

4. Mix the cocoa powder, baking powder, cinnamon and salt together, then add to the bean mixture and process briefly until smooth.

5. Spoon into the prepared tin and spread in an even layer. Bake in the preheated oven for about 25 minutes, or until the cake is well risen, beginning to crack around the edges and still slightly soft in the centre.

6. Sprinkle with the remaining chocolate chips and leave to cool for 20 minutes. Lift the paper and brownies out of the tin and transfer to a wire rack to cool completely. Cut into 16 small pieces, lift off the paper and serve or store in a tin for up to 2 days.

PER BROWNIE: *227 Kcals / 10.8g fat / 6.9g sat fat / 30g carbs / 21g sugar / 6.5g fibre / 5.7g protein / 0.5g salt*

Tofu Lemon Cheesecake

Serves 10

Prep: 30–35 minutes, plus chilling
Cook: 5 minutes

Base

125 g/4½ oz pecan nuts
175 g/6 oz soft dried dates
85 g/3 oz gingernut biscuits
2 tbsp agave syrup

Filling

350 g/12 oz firm silken tofu
300 g/10½ oz full-fat cream cheese
100 g/3½ oz Greek-style natural yogurt
juice and grated zest of 3 lemons,
  plus 1 tbsp zest to decorate
100 g/3½ oz soft light brown sugar
½ tsp vanilla extract
15 g/½ oz powdered gelatine
75 ml/2½ fl oz cold water

Fibre-filled dates and naturally sweet agave syrup add flavour and appeal to the crunchy ginger biscuit base, then zesty lemons add the finest refreshing flavour to the topping of this top-notch chilled cheesecake.

1. Line a 20-cm/8-inch round springform baking tin with baking paper.

2. To make the base, place the pecans, dates, biscuits and agave syrup in a food processor and pulse until the mixture comes together. The mixture should be slightly sticky when rolled in your hands. Empty the crust into the bottom of your prepared tin and press down to create an even base.

3. To make the filling, drain any excess water from the tofu and place in a food processor with the cream cheese, yogurt, lemon juice, lemon zest, brown sugar and vanilla extract. Blend until silky smooth.

4. Place the powdered gelatine in a small bowl and pour over the cold water. Set the bowl over a saucepan full of gently simmering water. Stir the gelatine until it has dissolved into the liquid and, working quickly, pour the liquid gelatine into the filling mixture. Blend the filling again until the gelatine is fully incorporated.

5. Spoon the filling on top of the base and place in the refrigerator to chill for 6 hours or overnight. Serve in slices, decorated with lemon zest.

PER SERVING: 368 Kcals / 22.2g fat / 7.7g sat fat / 37.6g carbs / 29.7g sugar / 2.9g fibre / 8.4g protein / 0.4g salt

Avocado Chocolate Mousse

Low in sugar, high in heart-friendly monounsaturated fat and suitable for vegetarians, this gorgeous, silken mousse is served in small portions as each spoonful packs a powerful creamy chocolate flavour.

Serves 4

Prep: 20 minutes
Cook: No cooking

2 ripe avocados, roughly chopped
35 g/1¼ oz cocoa powder
2 tbsp rice malt syrup
1 tsp vanilla extract
pinch of sea salt
2 tbsp unsweetened almond milk

1. Put all the ingredients in a blender or food processor and process until combined. Scrape down the sides and process for a further minute, or until the mousse is airy. If it is still too thick, add a splash more almond milk and process again briefly.

2. Spoon the mousse into small teacups or serving bowls and serve immediately. Alternatively, you can cover and chill the mousses in the refrigerator for up to 4 hours.

PER SERVING: *233 Kcals / 16g fat / 2.8g sat fat / 25.8g carbs / 9.2g sugar / 9.6g fibre / 3.7g protein / 0.4g salt*

Skinny Banana Split Sundaes

Serves 2

Prep: 20 minutes,
  plus freezing and cooling
Cook: 8–10 minutes

2 small bananas, roughly chopped
6 unblanched almonds,
  roughly chopped

Chocolate sauce

30 g/1 oz soft light brown sugar
3 tbsp cocoa powder
6 tbsp semi-skimmed milk
30 g/1 oz 70% plain chocolate,
  broken into pieces
½ tsp vanilla extract

There's nothing childish about these reduced-fat desserts. The naturally sweet ripe bananas are low in fat and rich in vitamins, minerals and fibre, so they produce the perfect frozen ice to accompany a sumptuous chocolate sauce.

1. Put the bananas in a plastic container and freeze for 2 hours. Transfer to a food processor and process until smooth and creamy. Return to the container, re-cover and freeze for 1 hour, or until firm.

2. To make the chocolate sauce, put the sugar, cocoa powder and milk into a small saucepan and bring to a simmer over a medium heat. Reduce the heat to low and cook, stirring constantly, for about 1 minute, or until the sugar and cocoa powder have dissolved.

3. Remove from the heat, then stir in the chocolate until it has melted. Stir in the vanilla extract. Leave the mixture to cool slightly.

4. Place a dry frying pan over a high heat. Add the almonds, cover and dry-fry for 3–4 minutes, or until toasted.

5. Scoop the banana purée into two glasses or bowls, drizzle with the warm chocolate sauce and sprinkle with the almonds.

Chia Seed & Banana Ice Lollies

Chia seeds are a rich source of omega-3 fatty acids and a good source of vitamins, minerals, protein and fibre. Combined with bananas, honey and yogurt, they create these sensational full-of-goodness ice lollies.

Makes 6

Prep: 20 minutes, plus freezing
Cook: No cooking

3 large, ripe bananas
3 tbsp Greek-style natural yogurt
2 tsp runny honey
2 tsp chia seeds

You will also need:

6 x 50 ml /2 fl oz ice lolly moulds
6 ice lolly sticks

1. Blend the bananas, Greek yogurt and honey in a blender or food processor until you have a thick, smooth consistency. Stir in the chia seeds.

2. Transfer the mixture to a jug and pour the mixture evenly into the six ice lolly moulds.

3. Place a lolly stick in the centre of each mould. Place in the freezer and leave to freeze for 6 hours before serving.

4. To unmould the lollies, dip the frozen moulds into warm water for a few seconds and gently release the lollies while holding the sticks.

PER LOLLY: *84 Kcals / 1.2g fat / 0.5g sat fat / 18.5g carbs / 10.6g sugar / 2.3g fibre / 1.9g protein / trace salt*

Chai Tea Biscuits

Makes 30
Prep: 25–30 minutes,
  plus chilling and cooling
Cook: 18–20 minutes

100 g/3½ oz soft light brown sugar
2 tbsp dry chai tea (about 4 teabags)
¼ tsp salt
125 g/4½ oz wholemeal plain flour
1 tsp vanilla extract
115 g/4 oz cold, unsalted butter
2 tbsp wholemeal plain flour, for dusting

Spicy, pungent, antioxidant-rich chai tea adds delicious flavour to these fibre-filled biscuits that provide a healthy, crunchy treat when you crave something sweet. They keep well for a few days too.

1. Preheat the oven to 180°C/350°F/ Gas Mark 4 and line a baking tray with baking paper.

2. Put the brown sugar, tea and salt into a food processor and whizz until the tea has been ground to a fine powder. Add the flour, vanilla extract and butter and process until well combined and the mixture begins to hold together. If the mixture is too dry, add cold water, ½ teaspoon at a time, and whizz until the mixture just comes together.

3. Turn out the dough on to a sheet of clingfilm and shape into a log. Wrap tightly and refrigerate for 15 minutes.

4. Roll out the dough on a lightly floured surface to about 3 mm/⅛ inch thick and cut into rounds, using a round 6-cm/2½-inch biscuit cutter (or use the shape of your choice). Transfer the biscuits to the prepared baking tray and bake in the preheated oven for 18–20 minutes, or until they begin to turn golden at the edges.

5. Remove from the oven and transfer the biscuits to a wire rack to cool completely.

PER BISCUIT: 58 Kcals / 3.2g fat / 2g sat fat / 7g carbs / 3.3g sugar / 0.5g fibre / 0.7g protein / trace salt

Coconut & Mango Quinoa Puddings

Serves 4

Prep: 20 minutes,
  plus standing and cooling
Cook: 15–20 minutes

300 ml/10 fl oz canned coconut milk
115 g/4 oz quinoa, rinsed
350 g/12 oz mango flesh,
  roughly chopped
75 g/2¾ oz golden caster sugar
juice of 1 large lime
4-cm/1½-inch piece fresh
  ginger, cut into chunks
100 g/3½ oz blueberries
4 tbsp toasted dried coconut shavings

Enjoy the fragrant flavours of this dairy-free dessert and benefit from the antioxidant goodness of fresh mango and blueberries.

1. Put the coconut milk and quinoa in a small saucepan and bring to the boil over a high heat. Reduce the heat to low, cover and simmer for 10–15 minutes, or until most of the liquid has evaporated. Remove from the heat and set aside for 7 more minutes to allow the grains to swell. Fluff up with a fork, tip into a bowl and leave to cool.

2. Meanwhile, put the mango, sugar and lime juice in a food processor. Squeeze the ginger through a garlic press and add the juice to the food processor. Process for 30 seconds, or until you have a smooth purée.

3. Mix the mango purée into the cooled quinoa, then cover and leave to stand for 30 minutes.

4. Spoon the mixture into four small bowls and sprinkle with the blueberries and coconut shavings. Serve immediately.

PER SERVING: *425 Kcals / 20.4g fat / 16.4g sat fat / 59.5g carbs / 35.5g sugar / 4.7g fibre / 6.8g protein / trace salt*

Mocha Soufflés with Mascarpone

You don't need to skimp on dessert with these luscious low-sugar soufflés. Crammed with vitamins, minerals and heart-healthy monounsaturated fat, ground almonds add goodness to these very tempting baked desserts.

Serves 4
Prep: 25–30 minutes, plus cooling
Cook: 18–20 minutes

2 tsp butter, to grease
2 tbsp ground almonds
1 tbsp cocoa powder
1 tbsp prepared strong espresso
pinch of sea salt
5 tbsp cold water
3 egg whites
1 tbsp rice malt syrup
1 tsp cocoa powder, to dust
4 tbsp mascarpone cheese, to serve

1. Preheat the oven to 190°C/375°F/Gas Mark 5. Lightly grease four ramekins, then sprinkle with the ground almonds. Roll and rotate the ramekins so the almonds stick to the butter, coating all sides.

2. Put the cocoa powder, espresso, salt and water in a small saucepan and cook, stirring over a low heat, until smooth. Increase the heat to medium–high and bring to the boil, then cook for a further 1 minute. Pour the mixture into a large bowl and leave to cool.

3. Put the egg whites in a separate large, clean grease-free bowl and whisk until they form soft peaks. Add the rice malt syrup and whisk again until you have stiff peaks. Using a metal spoon, gently fold a spoonful of the egg white into the cocoa mixture, preserving as much air as possible, then fold in the rest.

4. Spoon the mixture into the prepared ramekins. Bake for 10–12 minutes, or until the soufflés are towering out of the ramekins.

5. Add a tablespoon of mascarpone to each ramekin and sprinkle with cocoa powder. Serve immediately, before the soufflés start to collapse.

PER SERVING: *156 Kcals / 12g fat / 7.5g sat fat / 8.7g carbs / 5.4g sugar / 0.8g fibre / 4.4g protein / 0.5g salt*

Spiced Apple Wholemeal Cupcakes

Makes 12
Prep: 35–40 minutes, plus cooling
Cook: 50 minutes–1¼ hours

3 dessert apples
finely grated zest and juice of 1 lemon
85 g/3 oz wholemeal plain flour
85 g/3 oz brown rice flour
2 tsp baking powder
½ tsp ground mixed spice
115 g/4 oz unsalted butter,
    softened and diced
115 g/4 oz light muscovado sugar
2 eggs, beaten
225 ml/8 fl oz crème fraîche
¼ tsp ground mixed spice, to decorate

For a healthy sweet snack during the day or after a meal, opt for these appealing wholemeal apple cupcakes that are topped with lightly spiced crème fraîche and finished with a flurry of baked apple slices.

1. To make the apple sauce, peel, core and roughly chop two of the apples, then put them in a saucepan. Add the lemon zest and half of the juice. Cover and cook over a low heat for 5–10 minutes, or until soft. Mash until smooth, then leave to cool. Preheat the oven to 180°C/350°F/Gas Mark 4.

2. Put 12 paper cases or squares of baking paper in a 12-hole muffin tin. Put the wholemeal and rice flours, baking powder and mixed spice in a small bowl and mix well.

3. Cream the butter and sugar together in a large bowl. Beat in alternate spoonfuls of the eggs and the flour mixture until it is all used up, then stir in 150 g/5½ oz apple sauce (reserve any remaining for another time).

4. Spoon the mixture evenly into the paper cases. Bake for 15–18 minutes, or until well risen and the tops spring back when pressed with a fingertip. Leave to cool for 5 minutes, then transfer to a wire rack to cool completely.

5. Line a baking sheet with baking paper. Put the rest of the lemon juice in a medium bowl. Thinly slice the remaining apple, toss it in the lemon juice, then arrange it on the prepared baking sheet. Reduce the oven temperature to 110°C/225°F/Gas Mark ¼ and cook the apple slices, turning once, for 30–45 minutes, or until just beginning to brown. Turn off the oven and leave the apples to cool inside it. Lift off the slices with a palette knife and cut them in half.

6. Top each cupcake with a spoonful of crème fraîche, sprinkle with mixed spice and put two apple slice halves on top.

PER CUPCAKE: *244 Kcals / 14.8g fat / 9.3g sat fat / 26.1g carbs / 14g sugar / 1.7g fibre / 3.1g protein / 0.2g salt*

Gluten & Dairy-Free Orange & Almond Cake

Serves 8

Prep: 30 minutes, plus cooling
Cook: 2 hours 35 minutes–
  3 hours 5 minutes

375 g/13 oz oranges
  (approximately 2 small oranges)
10 g/¼ oz olive oil, to grease
6 eggs
225 g/8 oz muscovado sugar
250 g/9 oz ground almonds
1 tsp gluten-free baking powder
½ tsp ground cloves

Fig topping

4 plump figs, cut into segments
30 g/1 oz sliced almonds, toasted
zest of 1 orange

A real sweet treat for those following a gluten or dairy-free diet, this deliciously moist cake is packed with nourishing ground almonds and juicy fresh oranges, then served with a fabulous fig topping.

1. Place the oranges in a large saucepan with some cold water. Bring to a gentle simmer and cook for 1½–2 hours. Drain and, when cool, cut each orange in half and remove the pips. Put the oranges – skins, pith, fruit and all – into a blender or food processor and blitz.

2. Preheat the oven to 190°C/375°F/Gas Mark 5. Grease and line a 20-cm/8-inch round springform cake tin.

3. Place the eggs in a mixing bowl and gently beat them with a whisk. Add the sugar, almonds, baking powder and ground cloves to the bowl. Mix well before stirring through the pulped oranges.

4. Pour the mixture into the prepared tin and bake for 1 hour in the preheated oven, or until golden and a skewer inserted in the centre comes out clean. Remove from the oven and leave to cool in the tin on a wire rack. Once the cake is completely cool, remove from the tin.

5. Decorate the cake with the fresh figs, toasted almonds and the fresh orange zest.

PER SERVING: *409 Kcals / 23.3g fat / 2.8g sat fat / 42.4g carbs / 35.3g sugar / 4.9g fibre / 12.7g protein / 0.3g salt*

Fruity Ice Lollies

Fresh mango and strawberries, heaped with healthy vitamins, add wonderful colour and flavour to these easy-to-make iced yogurt treats. Sweetened naturally with honey, these low-fat lollies can be enjoyed by all the family.

Makes 8

Prep: 30 minutes, plus freezing
Cook: No cooking

325 g/11½ oz mango flesh
9 tbsp runny honey
300 ml/10 fl oz natural yogurt
2 tsp vanilla extract
300 g/10½ oz strawberries, hulled

You will also need:

8 x 100 ml /3½ fl oz ice lolly moulds
8 ice lolly sticks

1. Put the mango in a blender or food processor and process to a purée. Transfer to a jug, add 3 tablespoons of honey and stir well.

2. Pour the mixture into 8 x 100 ml/3½ fl oz ice lolly moulds. Freeze for 2 hours, or until firm.

3. When the mango mixture is frozen, put the yogurt, vanilla extract and 3 tablespoons of honey in a bowl and stir well. Spoon this over the frozen mango mixture. Insert the ice lolly sticks and freeze for 2–3 hours, or until firm.

4. When the vanilla mixture is frozen, put the strawberries and remaining 3 tablespoons of honey in a blender and process to a purée. Sieve out the seeds with a fine metal sieve. Pour this over the frozen vanilla mixture and freeze for 2–3 hours, or until firm.

5. To unmould the lollies, dip the frozen moulds into warm water for a few seconds and gently release the lollies while holding the sticks.

PER LOLLY: 134 Kcals / 1.5g fat / 0.8g sat fat / 30.3g carbs / 28.7g sugar / 1.4g fibre / 2g protein / trace salt

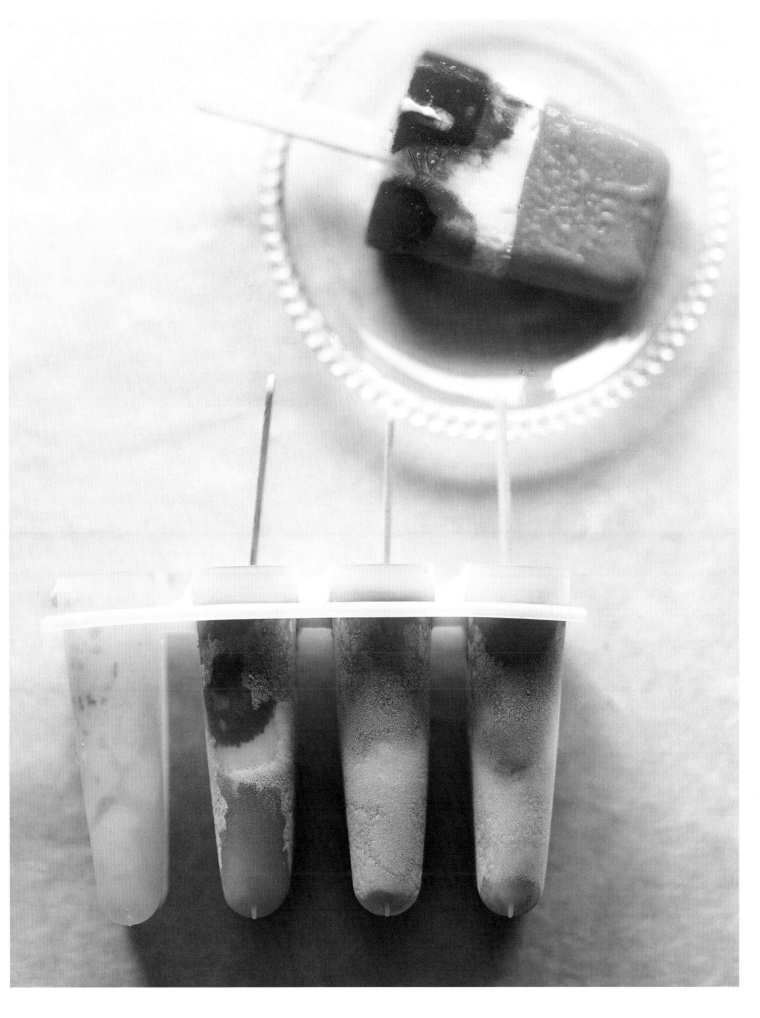

Summer Berry Sponge Cakes

Light and airy low-fat sponge cakes are topped with thick natural yogurt and a medley of mixed berries bursting with antioxidants, to create these delightful individual desserts, great for a gathering of family or friends.

Makes 6
Prep: 30 minutes, plus cooling
Cook: 12–15 minutes

1 tbsp olive oil, to grease
3 eggs
85 g/3 oz golden caster sugar
½ tsp vanilla extract
85 g/3 oz brown rice flour
250 g/9 oz low-fat Greek-style natural yogurt
150 g/5½ oz raspberries
150 g/5½ oz strawberries, hulled and sliced
100 g/3½ oz blueberries
1 tbsp icing sugar, sifted

1. Preheat the oven to 180°C/350°F/Gas Mark 4. Brush six 175-ml/6-fl oz ring mould tins with a little oil and put them on a baking sheet.

2. Put the eggs, caster sugar and vanilla extract in a large bowl and beat with an electric hand-held whisk for 5 minutes, or until the mixture is thick and leaves a trail when the whisk is lifted.

3. Sift the flour over the egg mixture, then gently fold it in with a large metal spoon. Spoon the mixture into the tins and ease it into an even layer, being careful not to knock out any air.

4. Bake in the preheated oven for 12–15 minutes, or until the cakes are risen and golden brown and beginning to shrink away from the edges.

5. Leave to cool in the tins for 5 minutes. Loosen the edges of the cakes with a round-bladed knife and turn them out onto a wire rack. Leave to cool completely.

6. Put the cakes on serving plates, spoon the yogurt into the centre, then pile the fruits on top. Dust with sifted icing sugar and serve immediately.

PER CAKE: 222 Kcals / 5.3g fat / 1.2g sat fat / 35.5g carbs / 21.4g sugar / 3.2g fibre / 9g protein / 0.1g salt

Raspberry & Watermelon Sorbet

Both refreshing and palate-cleansing, this fabulous fat-free fruit sorbet makes a lovely light dessert. Fresh raspberries and juicy watermelon ensure it's jam-packed with health-enhancing vitamins and minerals, especially vitamin C.

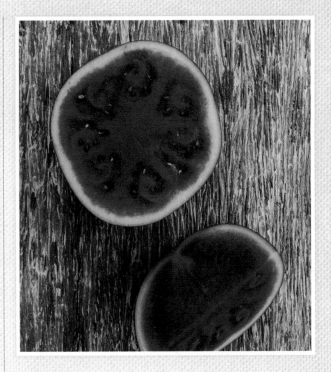

Serves 4
Prep: 30 minutes, plus cooling and freezing
Cook: 7–9 minutes

115 g/4 oz golden caster sugar
150 ml/5 fl oz cold water
finely grated zest and juice of 1 lime
225 g/8 oz raspberries
1 small watermelon, cut into chunks
1 egg white

1. Put the sugar, water and lime zest in a small saucepan and cook over a low heat, stirring, until the sugar has dissolved. Increase to high until the mixture comes to a boil, then reduce the heat to medium and simmer gently for 3–4 minutes. Leave the lime syrup to cool completely.

2. Put the raspberries and watermelon in a food processor in batches and process to a purée. Press the mixture through a sieve into a bowl to remove any remaining seeds.

3. Tip the purée into a loaf tin, pour in the lime syrup through a sieve, then stir in the lime juice. Freeze for 3–4 hours, or until the sorbet is beginning to freeze around the edges and the centre is still mushy.

4. Transfer the sorbet to a food processor and process to break up the ice crystals. Put the egg white in a small bowl and lightly whisk with a fork until frothy, then mix it into the sorbet.

5. Pour the sorbet into a plastic or metal container, cover and freeze for 3–4 hours, or until firm. Allow to soften at room temperature for 10–15 minutes before serving. Eat within a week of freezing.

PER SERVING: *232 Kcals / 0.8g fat / 0g sat fat / 57.7g carbs / 48.8g sugar / 4.9g fibre / 3.3g protein / trace salt*

Coconut, Cacao & Hazelnut Truffles

Makes 20
Prep: 25 minutes, plus storing
Cook: No cooking

85 g/3 oz unblanched hazelnuts
55 g/2 oz cacao nibs
6 dried soft figs, roughly chopped
25 g/1 oz desiccated coconut
1 tbsp maple syrup
finely grated zest and juice of
    ½ small orange
1 tbsp finely chopped cacao
    nibs, for coating
2 tbsp desiccated coconut, for coating

This super-charged and tasty power snack is crammed with natural ingredients, creating the perfect energy-giving pick-me-up.

1. Add the hazelnuts and the cacao nibs to a food processor and process until everything is very finely chopped.

2. Add the figs, coconut, maple syrup and orange zest and juice to the processor, and process until finely chopped and the mixture has come together in a ball.

3. Scoop the mixture out of the food processor, then cut into 20 even-sized pieces. Roll into small balls in your hands.

4. Mix the chopped cacao nibs with the coconut on a sheet of non-stick baking paper or a plate. Roll the truffles, one at a time, in the cacao and coconut mixture, then arrange in a small plastic container. Store in the refrigerator for up to 3 days.

PER TRUFFLE: *63 Kcals / 5g fat / 1.9g sat fat / 4.9g carbs / 2.6g sugar / 2g fibre / 1.3g protein / trace salt*

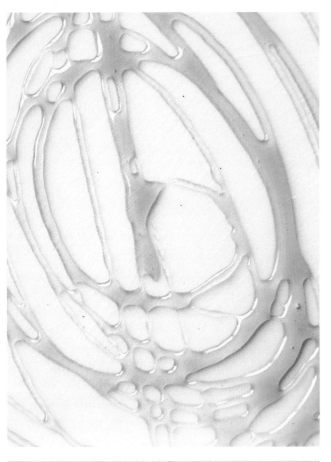

Chocolate & Chia Puddings

Coconut milk and natural yogurt add an appealing creaminess to these chilled chocolate puddings, plus agave syrup sweetens them naturally and on-trend chia seeds add that extra nutrient boost.

Serves 3

Prep: 20 minutes, plus chilling
Cook: No cooking

2 tbsp cocoa powder
2 tbsp agave syrup
90 ml/3 fl oz coconut milk
125 g/4½ oz Greek-style natural yogurt
2 tbsp chia seeds
1 tsp vanilla extract
1 kiwi, sliced, to decorate
50 g/1¾ oz plain chocolate, roughly chopped, to decorate

1. Place the cocoa powder and agave syrup in a large bowl and mix well to remove any lumps. Stir in the coconut milk, Greek yogurt, chia seeds and vanilla extract and mix thoroughly.

2. Cover and refrigerate for 4–6 hours. Remove the mixture from the refrigerator; it should be quite thick at this stage. Using an electric hand-held blender, whizz the mixture until smooth and carefully divide between three small dessert glasses.

3. Chill the puddings for a further hour. Decorate with the kiwi slices and plain chocolate and serve.

PER SERVING: *307 Kcals / 18.8g fat / 11.8g sat fat / 29.4g carbs / 18.7g sugar / 7g fibre / 7.9g protein / trace salt*

Celebration Chocolate & Beetroot Cake

Serves 8

Prep: 35–40 minutes, plus cooling
Cook: 1½ hours

10 g/¼ oz unsalted butter, for greasing
2 raw beetroot (approximately
    200 g/7 oz), cut into cubes
150 g/5½ oz plain chocolate with
    70% cocoa, broken into pieces
25 g/1 oz unsweetened cocoa powder
2 tsp baking powder
115 g/4 oz wholemeal plain flour
55 g/2 oz brown rice flour
200 g/7 oz unsalted butter,
    softened and diced
215 g/7½ oz light muscovado sugar
4 eggs
2 tbsp milk
300 ml/10 fl oz double cream

Fresh beetroot adds delicious natural sweetness to this indulgent chocolate cake and keeps it wonderfully moist too. This special occasion wholemeal cake will soon become a firm favourite for all committed chocoholics.

1. Preheat the oven to 160°C/325°F/ Gas Mark 3. Lightly grease a 20-cm/8-inch round springform cake tin and line with baking paper.

2. Half-fill the base of a steamer with water, bring to the boil, then put the beetroot in the steamer top. Cover with a lid and steam for 15 minutes, or until tender. Transfer the beetroot to a food processor and add 4 tablespoons of water from the base of the steamer. Purée until smooth, then leave to cool.

3. Put 115 g/4 oz of the chocolate in a heatproof bowl set over a saucepan of gently simmering water, ensuring the bowl doesn't touch the water. Leave for 5 minutes, or until the chocolate has melted.

4. Sift the cocoa into a second bowl, then stir in the baking powder and wholemeal and rice flours.

5. Cream the butter and 200 g/7 oz sugar together in a large bowl. Beat in the eggs, one by one, adding spoonfuls of the flour mixture between each egg and beating well after each addition. Stir in the remaining flour mixture, the puréed beetroot and melted chocolate, and beat until smooth, then mix in enough of the milk to make a soft dropping consistency.

6. Spoon the mixture into the prepared tin and spread it into an even layer. Bake for 1 hour, or until well risen, the top is slightly cracked and a skewer comes out cleanly when inserted into the centre of the cake. Leave to cool for 15 minutes, then remove from the tin, peel off the baking paper and transfer the cake to a wire rack.

7. To finish, melt the remaining chocolate in a heatproof bowl set over a saucepan of gently simmering water, ensuring the bowl doesn't touch the water. Put the cream in a bowl, add the remaining sugar and whisk until soft swirls form. Cut the cake in half and put the bottom half on a serving plate. Spoon one-third of the cream mixture onto the base of the cake, add the top half of the cake, then spoon the remaining cream on the top. Drizzle with the melted chocolate and serve.

PER SERVING: *662 Kcals / 46.6g fat / 27.9g sat fat / 56.5g carbs / 32.8g sugar / 5.6g fibre / 9.2g protein / 0.5g salt*

Passion Fruit & Strawberry Yogurts

Passion fruit and strawberries add vibrant colour and vital vitamins to these zesty single portion yogurt desserts. Each one is finished with a sprinkling of nutrient-rich dried goji berries for a further nutritious lift.

Serves 4

Prep: 20–25 minutes, plus cooling and chilling
Cook: 2–3 minutes

20 g/¾ oz desiccated coconut
200 g/7 oz strawberries, hulled
finely grated zest and juice of 1 lime
350 g/12 oz low-fat Greek-style natural yogurt
4 tsp runny honey
2 passion fruit, halved
1 tbsp dried goji berries, roughly chopped

1. Add the coconut to a dry frying pan and cook over a medium heat for 2–3 minutes, shaking the pan, until light golden in colour. Remove the coconut from the heat and leave to cool.

2. Roughly mash the strawberries and mix with half of the lime juice.

3. Add the lime zest, remaining lime juice, the yogurt and honey to a bowl, and stir together. Add three quarters of the cooled coconut to the yogurt, then scoop the seeds from the passion fruit over the top and lightly fold into the yogurt.

4. Layer alternate spoonfuls of strawberry and yogurt in 4 x 200-ml/7-fl oz preserving jars, then sprinkle with the remaining coconut and the goji berries. Clip down the lids and chill until ready to serve. Eat within 24 hours.

PER SERVING: 139 Kcals / 3.5g fat / 2.8g sat fat / 18.9g carbs / 14.5g sugar / 3g fibre / 10g protein / 0.1g salt

Healthy Nectars

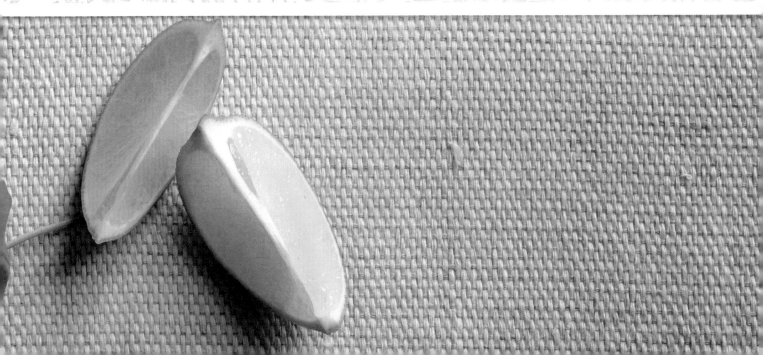

Ruby Fruit Reviving Smoothie

Serves 1

Prep: 15 minutes
Cook: No cooking

1 ruby red grapefruit, zest and
   a little pith removed, deseeded
   and roughly chopped
¼ cucumber, roughly chopped
150 g/5½ oz strawberries, hulled
small handful of crushed ice, optional

Simple to make, this scrumptious smoothie, full of vitamin C, is guaranteed to get you off to a great start in the morning.

1. Place the grapefruit and cucumber in a blender and whizz until smooth.

2. Add the strawberries and crushed ice, if using, and whizz until blended.

3. Pour the smoothie into a glass and serve immediately.

PER SERVING: *162 Kcals / 0.8g fat / 0g sat fat / 40.4g carbs / 25.5g sugar / 7.3g fibre / 3.4g protein / trace salt*

Melon & Coconut Mock Mojito

Promote your general health and well-being with this vivid green mock mojito. It's loaded with nourishing nutrients and can be whizzed up in minutes, providing the essential energy boost needed after a workout.

Serves 1
Prep: 15–20 minutes
Cook: No cooking

20 g/¾ oz spinach
50 g/1¾ oz coconut flesh
200 ml/7 fl oz chilled water
100 g/3½ oz cantaloupe melon, peeled, deseeded and chopped
1 tbsp chopped fresh mint
juice of ½ lime
50 g/1¾ oz mango, peeled, stoned and
    chopped, plus 1 extra slice to decorate
crushed ice, to serve, optional

1. Place the spinach, coconut and water in a blender and whizz until smooth.

2. Add the melon, mint, lime juice and mango, and blend until smooth and creamy.

3. Pour over crushed ice, if using, and serve immediately, decorated with a mango slice.

PER SERVING: 262 Kcals / 17.2g fat / 14.9g sat fat / 28g carbs / 20.3g sugar / 7.3g fibre / 3.9g protein / trace salt

Kale, Lettuce & Avocado Juice

Serves 1
Prep: 20 minutes
Cook: No cooking

55 g/2 oz kale
30 g/1 oz fresh flat-leaf parsley
½ romaine or cos lettuce
3 celery sticks, halved
1 apple, halved
½ lemon
30 g/1 oz flaked almonds
½ avocado, peeled and stoned
small handful of crushed ice, optional

Get a good helping of fruit and vegetables in a glass with this fabulous fresh juice that is ideal for anyone needing a boost. The flaked almonds add a beneficial bonus of heart-healthy monounsaturated fat, plus vitamin E.

1. Feed the kale through a juicer, followed by the parsley and lettuce. Finally, feed two of the celery sticks and the apple and lemon through the juicer.

2. Put the flaked almonds in a blender or food processor and process until finely ground.

3. Add the juice and avocado flesh to the almonds, and process until smooth. Add the crushed ice, if using, and blend again.

4. Pour the juice into a glass. Decorate with the remaining celery stick and serve immediately.

PER SERVING: *441 Kcals / 31.6g fat / 3.3g sat fat / 35.3g carbs / 14.2g sugar / 9.8g fibre / 13.9g protein / 0.3g salt*

Spinach & Melon Cooler

Serves 1

Prep: 15 minutes
Cook: No cooking

½ Galia melon, peeled, deseeded
  and thickly sliced
85 g/3 oz baby spinach
2 large stems of fresh
  flat-leaf parsley
3 large stems of fresh mint
small handful of ice, optional

Antioxidant-rich spinach and vitamin-packed Galia melon create this cleansing cooler, enhanced with the addition of fresh garden herbs. It's great as a refreshing fat-free drink when your body needs reinvigorating.

1. Feed the melon through a juicer, followed by the spinach, parsley and two stems of the mint.

2. Half-fill a glass with ice, if using, then pour in the juice.

3. Decorate with the remaining stem of mint and serve immediately.

Vegetable Stomach Soothing Juice

To keep your tummy in tip-top health, choose this appealing vegetable stomach soother, which is enriched with a little hemp seed oil that adds an important boost of polyunsaturated fat and vitamin E.

Serves 1

Prep: 20 minutes
Cook: No cooking

3 oranges, zest and a little pith removed
1 carrot, halved
2 tomatoes, roughly chopped
125 ml/4 fl oz chilled water
1 small green chilli, halved
2 celery sticks, thickly sliced
2 tsp hemp seed oil

1. Cut two oranges in half and feed them and the carrot through a juicer. Pour the juice into a blender.

2. Roughly chop and deseed the remaining orange, then place it, the tomatoes and water into the blender and whizz until smooth.

3. Add the chilli and celery and whizz again until blended. Pour the juice into a glass, stir in the hemp seed oil and serve immediately.

PER SERVING: *302 Kcals / 10.5g fat / 1.4g sat fat / 50.3g carbs / 37.1g sugar / 8g fibre / 5.8g protein / 0.1g salt*

Broccoli & Parsley Revitalizing Juice

Serves 1

Prep: 15 minutes
Cook: No cooking

115 g/4 oz broccoli,
    broken into large florets
30 g/1 oz fresh flat-leaf parsley
½ fennel bulb
2 apples, halved
chilled water, to taste, optional
small handful of ice, optional

After a weekday workout or some strenuous exercise, this vitamin and mineral-loaded juice is guaranteed to revitalize your body quickly. It's also fat-free and free of processed sugars, making it a great alternative to fizzy energy drinks.

1. Feed the broccoli and parsley through the juicer, followed by the fennel and apples.

2. Top up the juice with chilled water to taste, if desired.

3. Half-fill a glass with ice, if using, then pour in the juice. Serve the juice immediately.

PER SERVING: *119 Kcals / 0.6g fat / 0g sat fat / 27g carbs / 15.1g sugar / 0.2g fibre / 3.2g protein / 0.2g salt*

Sprout Tonic

Serves 1
Prep: 10 minutes
Cook: No cooking

75 g/2¾ oz Brussels sprouts
25 g/1 oz beetroot leaves
30 g/1 oz chard
250 ml/9 fl oz unsweetened rice milk

Brussels sprouts boast vitamins, minerals, fibre and protein in this intense health-giving tonic that is appetizing and satisfying.

1. Place the Brussels sprouts, beetroot leaves and chard in a blender or food processor.

2. Pour the rice milk into the blender or food processor and blend until smooth and creamy.

3. Pour the tonic into a glass and serve immediately.

PER SERVING: 162 Kcals / 2.7g fat / 0g sat fat / 31.8g carbs / 15.2g sugar / 5g fibre / 4.2g protein / 0.5g salt

Warm Rocket, Apple & Ginseng Juice

Serves 1
Prep: 10 minutes, plus infusing
Cook: No cooking

1 ginseng tea bag or 1 tsp ginseng looseleaf tea
150 ml/5 fl oz boiling water
1 apple, halved
40 g/1½ oz rocket

1. Place the tea bag or ginseng tea in a cup. Pour the boiling water over the top and leave the mixture to infuse for about 4 minutes. Strain the tea into a handled glass or mug.

2. Feed the apple through a juicer, followed by the rocket.

3. Stir the juice into the tea in the glass and serve while it is still warm.

This revitalizing drink can also be enjoyed cold. Simply leave to cool, then drop in some ice cubes and stir well before serving.

PER SERVING: 48 Kcals / 0.3g fat / 0g sat fat / 10.4g carbs / 7.6g sugar / 0.1g fibre / 1.1g protein / trace salt

Protein Berry Whip

Serves 4

Prep: 10–15 minutes

Cook: No cooking

200 g/7 oz frozen sliced strawberries

55 g/2 oz frozen blueberries

40 g/1½ oz Brazil nuts

40 g/1½ oz cashew nuts, chopped

25 g/1 oz porridge oats

450 ml/16 fl oz almond milk

2 tbsp maple syrup

1. Place the strawberries, blueberries, Brazil nuts and cashew nuts in a blender. Sprinkle over the oats, then pour in half of the almond milk. Blend until smooth.

2. Add the remaining milk and maple syrup, and blend again until smooth.

3. Pour the berry whip into four glasses and serve immediately with spoons. As the drink stands, the blueberries will almost set the liquid, but as soon as you stir it, it will turn to liquid again.

These whips contain good amounts of protein, which is essential for the growth and repair of muscles and helps to fight infection.

PER SERVING: *209 Kcals / 12.8g fat / 2.4g sat fat / 21.5g carbs / 10.4g sugar / 3.6g fibre / 5g protein / 0.1g salt*

Bee Pollen & Nectarine Milkshake

Nutritious bee pollen adds an intriguing touch to this nifty and nourishing nectarine milkshake. Milk and natural yogurt team up to create a calcium-rich base, and the honey adds natural sweetness too.

Serves 2

Prep: 15 minutes
Cook: No cooking

2 ripe nectarines, quartered
200 ml/7 fl oz semi-skimmed milk
2 tbsp Greek-style natural yogurt
1 tbsp bee pollen
1 tsp runny honey
handful of ice cubes
1 tsp bee pollen, to decorate
2 slices nectarine, to decorate

1. Place the the nectarines, milk, yogurt, bee pollen and honey in a blender and whizz until smooth. Add the ice cubes and whizz again until completely blended.

2. Pour the milkshake into chilled glasses and decorate with the bee pollen and a fresh slice of nectarine. Serve immediately.

PER SERVING: 163 Kcals / 3.2g fat / 1.8g sat fat / 28.7g carbs / 22.8g sugar / 2.6g fibre / 7.3g protein / 0.1g salt

Raw Cocoa Milkshake

Great for waking up your taste buds first thing, or for a nutritious chocolate hit any time, this delicious dairy-free and gluten-free milkshake provides the perfect pick-me-up that is suitable for vegetarians and vegans too.

Serves 4

Prep: 10 minutes
Cook: No cooking

400 ml/14 fl oz almond milk
85 g/3 oz dried dates
85 g/3 oz cashew nuts
2 tbsp raw cocoa powder
1 tsp ground cinnamon
handful of ice cubes
1 tbsp orange zest, to decorate

1. Place the almond milk, dates, cashew nuts, cocoa powder, cinnamon and ice into a blender.

2. Blend thoroughly until the milkshake is a thick pouring consistency.

3. Pour into chilled glasses, decorate with the orange zest and serve immediately.

PER SERVING: 198 Kcals / 10.8g fat / 2g sat fat / 24.9g carbs / 15.5g sugar / 3.9g fibre / 5.2g protein / 0.1g salt

Pineapple & Mint Iced Tea

This refreshing iced tea is infused with soothing ginger and fresh mint and delivers a bounty of vitamins and minerals, ensuring a fresh, rejuvenating drink that is quenching at any time of the day.

Makes 500 ml/18 fl oz
Prep: 20–25 minutes, plus infusing
Cook: 45 minutes

1 pineapple
1 litre/1¾ pints water
30 g/1 oz fresh mint sprigs
5-cm/2-inch piece of fresh ginger, finely sliced
125 ml/4 fl oz agave syrup
crushed ice
2 tbsp mint leaves, to decorate

1. Prepare the pineapple by slicing off the base and leaves with a sharp knife. Rest the pineapple on its base and slice off the peel, until you reveal the flesh. Slice the fruit in half and remove the woody core that sits down the centre. Cut the remaining flesh into 2-cm/¾-inch cubes.

2. Pour the water into a large saucepan and add the pineapple, mint and ginger. Stir in the agave syrup and place the saucepan over a medium–high heat. Simmer for 45 minutes, or until the liquid has reduced by half.

3. Remove from the heat and allow the nectar to cool completely and infuse. This will take 4–5 hours. Using a slotted spoon, remove the mint sprigs and ginger.

4. Empty the crushed ice into the bottom of a large jug and add the fresh mint leaves. Pour over the cooled nectar and stir to mix. Serve immediately.

PER 500 ML/18 FL OZ: *810 Kcals / 1.2g fat / 0.1g sat fat / 206.8g carbs / 177.1g sugar / 13.5g fibre / 5.3g protein / trace salt*

Kiwi & Cucumber Infused Water

Makes 1.5 litres / 2¾ pints
Prep: 20 minutes, plus freezing
Cook: No cooking

½ cucumber
2 kiwis, peeled and thickly sliced
1 litre/1¾ pints chilled water

Lemon ice cubes

zest of 1 lemon
water to fill an ice-cube tray

Chilled water is infused with kiwi and cucumber to make this cleansing and refreshing drink. Served with zesty lemon ice cubes, it is a great thirst-quencher, especially when you're feeling hot and tired.

1. Make your lemon ice cubes at least 4 hours before they are needed. Cut the lemon zest into pieces that will sit neatly in the holes of an ice-cube tray. Place the zest pieces in the holes of the tray and fill the holes with water. Freeze for at least 4–6 hours, or until needed.

2. When ready to serve, peel ribbons from a cucumber using a vegetable peeler. Place the ribbons in the bottom of a jug, along with the fresh kiwi slices.

3. Add the lemon zest ice cubes to the jug and top up with the chilled water. Serve immediately.

PER 1.5 L/2¾ PINTS: *110 Kcals / 0.9g fat / 0.1g sat fat / 26.7g carbs / 15.1g sugar / 5.5g fibre / 2.7g protein / trace salt*

Cardamom, Fennel & Ginger Tea

Get your day off to a great start with this fragrant and soothing low-sugar tea, infused with spices. Ginger is a helpful digestive aid and has important anti-inflammatory properties, adding to this beneficial hot tea.

Makes 1 litre/1¾ pints
Prep: 10–15 minutes, plus infusing
Cook: No cooking

10 green cardamom pods
1 tsp fennel seeds
8-cm/3¼-inch piece of fresh ginger, sliced
1 litre/1¾ pints boiling water

1. Place the cardamom pods on a heavy chopping board and gently bruise each pod with a rolling pin.

2. Place the crushed pods into a teapot. Add the fennel seeds and fresh ginger. Pour the boiling water over the top and allow the tea to infuse for 5–6 minutes, or to your taste.

3. Pour the tea into mugs through a tea strainer and serve immediately.

PER 1 L/1¾ PINTS: *2 Kcals / 0g fat / 0g sat fat / 0.5g carbs / 0g sugar / 0.1g fibre / 0.1g protein / trace salt*

Homemade Masala Chai Tea

Makes 600 ml / 1 pint

Prep: 15 minutes

Cook: 30–35 minutes

1 tbsp Assam loose-leaf tea

5-cm/2-inch piece of
    fresh ginger, grated

2 cinnamon sticks

5 black peppercorns

6 cloves

5 green cardamom pods, bashed

2 star anise

300 ml/10 fl oz semi-skimmed milk

1 tbsp honey

Aromatic mixed spices, including ginger, cinnamon and cloves, add a lovely warming flavour to this restorative hot milky tea. It is naturally sweetened with honey, keeping it free from refined and processed sugar.

1. Place 300 ml/10 fl oz of water in a saucepan and bring to the boil over a medium heat. Stir in the Assam tea and continue to gently boil for 3–4 minutes.

2. Add the ginger, cinnamon sticks, peppercorns, cloves, cardamom and star anise and gently simmer for about 12–15 minutes. Add the milk and simmer for a further 10 minutes.

3. Sweeten with the honey. Strain the tea and serve immediately in mugs or tall glasses.

PER 600 ML/1 PINT: 217 Kcals / 5.9g fat / 3.8g sat fat / 32.5g carbs / 32.4g sugar / 0.2g fibre / 10g protein / 0.4g salt

315

INDEX